MORE PRAISE FOR "THREE RED SUITCASES"

The book was easy to read. Made me laugh and made me cry. Genuine. Authentic.

Nancy Brown, Culver City, California, Author of Foreword

I felt like I got to experience second-hand a childhood so different from my own. The author's account of her childhood experiences really changed my perception of life in the south, having only grown up hearing about stories in newspapers and on television.

Susan Teed, Vancouver Island, British Columbia, Canada

In the late 90's, I met Levonne when my family and I participated in a photo documentary exhibition she created of multi-ethnic families. Three Red Suitcases is a well-organized account of her own multi-ethnic family history and the tumultuous journey from school racial segregation to integration in the Southern United States during the 50's and 60's.

Peter Likins, Ph.D., President Emeritus of the University of Arizona

A heartfelt story of a white-looking girl living in a black world a generation before my birth. I couldn't put the book down.

Anna Batoosingh, Sonoma County, California

My passion for engaging, teaching and mentoring youth, particularly girls, was in full swing when I worked alongside Levonne at the Pascua Yaqui Tribe Charter High School in Tucson, Arizona. Her girlhood story is one of resiliency, confidence and strength of the human spirit.

Theresa Cariño, Co-founder/Executive Director Salud y Cariño

Three Red Suitcases is a compelling story of a girl caught between worlds and her search for self.

Joseph H. Nunn, Professor Emeritus, U.C.L.A.

Lovingly and humorously, Ms Gaddy challenges our assumptions about the human family. Her writing is filled with insight about the joys we reap in enhancing and blending cultures.

Bernice Roberts, Tucson, Arizona

I've known Levonne as a colleague, mentor, friend, and artist. Her commitment to living in deep integrity with herself, her friends and family, and her community grew out of her roots and ties to her family and rural North Carolina hometown. Levonne's book takes us through her upbringing to help us understood how her experiences shaped her.

Loretta Ishida, Baltimore, Maryland

Being a father, a brother, a friend, I felt helpless when I read about the girl in this book being violated by a relative. Her spunk made me cheer.

Larry Wallace, Durham, North Carolina

I was moved to laughter and tears by Levonne's heartbreaking and heroic story. The human spirit is truly marvelous!

Peggy Yeargain-Williams, Fountain Hills, Arizona

THREE RED SUITCASES

THREE RED SUITCASES

A Southern Childhood

LEVONNE GADDY

STAR LIGHT PUBLICATIONS

PARKSVILLE, BRITISH COLUMBIA, CANADA

Published by

Star Light Publications

P.O. Box 38

Parksville, BC, Canada V9P 2G3

www.LevonneGaddy.com

Library and Archives Canada Cataloging in Publication

Library of Congress Cataloging-in-Publication Data

Gaddy, Levonne

Three Red Suitcases: A Southern Childhood / Levonne Gaddy

ISBN 978-1-7753429-0-8

eISBN 978-1-7753429-1-5

Audio 978-1-7753429-2-2

1. Cultural, Ethnic, Regional/African American –

Autobiography. 2. Personal Memoir –
Autobiography. 3. Cultural, Ethnic, Regional/
Native American/Aboriginal—Autobiography. 4.
Dysfunctional families – Family and Relationships.
5. Prejudice – Family and Relationships. 6.
Domestic Partner Abuse—Family and
Relationships. 7. Death, Grief, Bereavement
–Family and Relationships. 8. North Carolina
–Social life and customs.

Cover design by Rush Kress

Cover art by Levonne Gaddy

Cover Author Photograph by Summer & Co. Photography

Bound and Printed in United States

DEDICATION

To my parents, Robert Lee Gaddy, Sr. and

Ovella Gaddy Tyson,

to their parents, and to all the ancestors.

Thank you for my inheritance.

To my brothers, Lee Gaddy,

Dale Gaddy, James Gaddy and Lewis Tyson.

FOREWORD

I met Levonne Gaddy in the early 1980's. She had invited people from Los Angeles, where we both lived at the time, to gather to speak about the wants and needs of multiracial families and people. Months later, she and I co-founded a support organization for this population – Multiracial Americans of Southern California (M.A.S.C). This was new and groundbreaking work at the time. Over the years since, we have remained colleagues and have deepened our friendship.

Levonne's story, *Three Red Suitcases*, brings the reader directly into her life during 1950's and 1960's rural North Carolina. It is engaging, sad, funny, poignant, and tragic. A mother/daughter journey at it's core, the story also reveals how she, as a mixed race person, and her multiracial family navigated life at a time when segregation and racism in the south was an ever-present reality.

Unpacking her story is an adventure that illuminates the life of the author from her childhood through her teenage years. It is a sweet and sad saga of family and friendship.

I hope you will journey with Levonne as she tries to understand her father's alcoholic anger and her mother's passivity, her sense of freedom when she's in nature, and the love of her siblings. The author's writing is specific and descriptive, as if painting a picture for the reader. The painting is not always pretty, as the author has to confront painful realities of death and sexual violations at a tender age.

As a therapist, I understand the healing that can happen through story-telling, both for the teller and the listener. I am hopeful others will experience catharsis and joy from my friend's universal story of love, grief, family, community and resilience.

Nancy Gundel Brown, Co-founder, Former President, and Current Board Member of Multiracial Americans of Southern California, Clinical Nurse Specialist, Kaiser Permanente

AUTHOR'S NOTES

How does one tell about a sixty-year process in a few paragraphs? This book began before I was born and continues through today. *Three Red Suitcases: A Southern Childhood* is a story of my growing up, and thus includes my family, my community, and the greater world that surrounded us at the time. The 1960's were tumultuous; as was my journey through that decade.

In the 1970's, I began a period of sorting out and beginning to heal from the Post Traumatic Stress (PTSD) that resulted from the negative elements in earlier years. Namely my parents' excessive alcohol use and their domestic partner abuse, along with traumas from my loss of a parent, child labor abuse, racism, integration of North Carolina schools, sexual assault, and poverty.

By the 1980's, I had fully engaged in transforming my trauma into doing what was within my power to help others heal. I trained and worked as a social worker and I honed my writing skills. My experience as a social worker showed me clearly that my family's problems were not limited to the six people that occupied my childhood home. Much of the world experienced something similar to at least one, often several, of the things that I and my family experienced. Our

1

little group of related-by-birth individuals absorbed and reflected back what was in the greater world around us. We were clearly and simply acting out our Oneness with all of Creation.

In my memoir, I have attempted to be as objective as I can, describing what I saw, heard, smelled, tasted, felt both physically and through emotions. At the time of writing, I followed Judith Barrington's guide for writing memoir in her book, *Writing the Memoir: From Truth to Art*. Her book was a first to guide the everyday person on how to write artfully about one's own life.

Based on today's norms for writing creative non-fiction, I have told only of things that actually happened, and that I witnessed myself. The exception to this rule is my stories about my parents' beginnings and their relationship before I was born. Those stories are based on oral history in our family, substantiated by census documents and other historical records that I was able to find to corroborate specific people at particular places in time.

To protect myself and my family, I have changed identifying information—including name, description, place, and occupation where I deemed necessary.

When more than one significant character in the story had the same name, I changed one of the names, to make it less confusing for the reader. I, at times, used the element of compositing, in order to create a more fluid, less cumbersome reading experience. The small community in Star, North Carolina, where I spent part of my youth, did not have a name. For ease in talking about it, I named it Dunn-

Green town. I hope those community members who still live there will appreciate my artistic license in this regard.

The writing of this book took every ounce of focus, energy, strength, and courage I could muster along the way. It has taken over a decade to bring it into full life so that I might release it back into the world from where the story originates. It has taken a similar degree of all those elements to edit, audio record, and make public this work of my lifetime. It is my dream that this piece of art, that I have done my best to shape, will entertain while stimulating healing for others. The sharing of these experiences must be my purpose on earth. Why else would such a childhood have been chosen?

Peace and Love, Levonne Gaddy

1

I leave my mother's seven sisters and brothers standing on the sidewalk along Troy, North Carolina's sedated Main Street. My husband John and I ignore the summer midday humidity as we walk toward the funeral parlor. I anticipate people's comments. Someone will say, "She looks as though she is sleeping peacefully." Another will say "Isn't she beautiful?" There will be comments about her hair, her make-up, the expression on her face, her clothes. I am ready for this. I have traveled one thousand miles from Arizona to North Carolina to see Mama. I need to see her. My husband, accustomed to cremation's quick reduction of flesh and bone to ashes, does not understand this need to be with my mother's body. I cannot explain it to him.

Dale, my younger brother, found our seventy-year-old mother dead in her front yard two days earlier. "I stopped by to check on Mama like I do most every day on my way home from work. I parked my truck on the road out front then walked all the way through her house calling 'Mama, where you at?' I couldn't find her. So I went back outside and stood on her front porch. I thought to myself, she must be out back. Just as I started down the steps, something caught me out the corner of my eye. Well, I looked over toward Mama's flower bed and there she was, lying curled up in a patch of purple lilies. She'd just been to my house the night before for supper."

Dale's wife Margo helped groom and dress my mother for this most special occasion of her last few days in view of others before being placed in the ground. Mama would be proud of the fuss and care taken for the honoring of her departure. Margo is inside the funeral home. She had said on the telephone, "Ovella was complaining of pain in her neck when she was at our house. We wondered if she had the flu. She fumbled with her cigarette trying to get it back into the pack before she drove off. Levonne, I didn't think anything of it really. She promised she'd go to the doctor the next day if she wasn't feeling better."

It had been Thanksgiving 2001, on a trip back to North Carolina, that I last saw or talked with my mother. I had spent eighteen months yearning for an answer to my cards or a call. After a lifetime of trying to drag more of a connection out of her, why was I expecting reciprocity to materialize in our relationship?

Inside, we learn that Mama is in the west room. We approach the door where the funeral director stands straight, looking serious, hands folded in front of him. I reach for the door's handle, ready to enter, eager. At the same moment of my reaching, the funeral director blocks our way.

"Family only," he says as though he is protecting a queen's tomb from grave looters. I suspect in a flash exactly what he is saying. I am angry in a flash. I know that what he means is that the family members of the woman in this room are black people and you two are white. I snap back, "That's my mother in there!" The funeral director apologizes and moves quickly aside.

I am angry all over. I tremble. I hate that at this most personal moment, the old issues of race surface. I am hurt. We enter the room where my thirty-year-old half-brother Lewis, who is seventeen years younger than me, stands crying and talking out loud. He is saying that he cannot believe that our mother is gone. He seems exaggerated to me, his response emotionally big, his tears and words unrestrained.

"Levonne, Levonne." Lewis calls out my name from his standing bent-over-at-the waist mourning position, "Can you believe it?" His tears flow so hard that I wonder how he can see that it's me. "Mama is gone." His words wash over me like a lone wolf's howl on the desert. "Mama is gone." I turn toward my mother's casket and am greeted with a long quiet hug from Margo, and then from Lewis' girlfriend, Sakina. They remain in place with John while I walk the ten or so steps to my mother.

I am allowed some moments alone to look at her, to touch her, to examine her in a way as one might examine a new baby for the first time. How do her hands look? Her lips? Her closed eyes? What does the expression on her face tell about her last moments on this earth as a living person? She seems small. I ask myself *Am I the same person that this woman tried to coax into touching my dead father's face as he lay in his casket more than three decades earlier?* The extreme difference between a child's revulsion of a dead body and my irrepressible draw to Mama's astounds me. I cannot take my eyes away from the woman who gave me life. I know that there will not be enough time for me with her. I know it and ache for it in the same instance.

The questions begin. Margo and Sakina take turns asking.

"Isn't she beautiful?"

"Do you like her hair?"

I want to say in response *She is dead! How can she be beautiful!?* But I do not. I know my approval of how my mother has been cared for in these final days is important. I know this so I say, "Yes, yes she looks wonderful. You have done a fine job with her. Thank you." In the comfort of Margo's hug, I feel envious that she has spent hours with my mother's body. I ache for those hours.

I want most of all to be alone with Mama but others come into the room. I am flooded with their expressions of caring, with comforting touches, words of love and astonishment that Mama seemed healthy one day and was gone the next. In the midst of my yearning, and everyone's needs, I realize that the holder of the memories of me as an infant is gone forever. I feel alone even with everyone around me. Pieces of my past and my future have in an instant slipped irretrievably and irrevocably away. I feel the strangeness of being parentless.

John and I leave the funeral home and drive toward my mother's house. My heart and my mind are full. In the warmth of the car under the June sun that lights the blue cloud-studded sky, I begin to recall. People say that your entire life flashes before you as you die. I would add that when an immediate family member dies, your life together flashes before you. At least that is what happened for me.

The flashes of my and my mother's life together, the recalling of my dead father, and the longing for time with Mama's body sets loose dormant wonderings about both my parents. Memories of a lonely childhood flood my mind. Beneath the loss and longing is a vague awareness that my life had been set on its course long before I was born.

∞

Lena Peoples, my mother's mother, my maternal grandmother, was the oldest of twelve siblings. As a young woman, she supervised her younger brothers' and sisters' work. Should any of her siblings fail to pick the established quota of cotton in the field in a day, clear the designated amount of land, or lay the acceptable number of railroad ties, Lena was the one held responsible by her father and was punished with a beating. His supervisory training had been learned from generations of colored slave foremen on North and South Carolina plantations.

Lena despised and feared her father. In the summer of 1930, she was briefly relieved of the responsibility for her siblings when she was hired out to the local widowed physician. She was to live on the doctor's farm and assist with house cleaning and cooking while the doctor's sixteen-year-old daughter-in-law, Sarah, lay sick and feverish from complications of a stillbirth.

Lena gathered soiled clothing and linens from the doc-

9

tor's home and from his son, Harvey, and Sarah's house next door. She fanned flies and heated water outdoors in black pots over wood fires. She put lye soap in the boiling water of one pot along with stained light-colored items.

As laundry steamed outside, Lena cooked the day's meals inside. She cooked everything slowly on the doctor's wood stove. Beans–pintos or navy—fresh collard greens, fried chicken or ham, and biscuits. The heat from the fire under the laundry pots and from the indoor wood stove added to the sticky heat of the August days.

On the third day of her new job, on her way to the back of the doctor's house, as she carried dried laundry from the clothesline, Lena ran into Harvey. He was her own age, nineteen, and three years older than his young wife, Sarah.

Lena's petite light-brown-skinned body had moved along lightly before crashing into Harvey. She bounced backwards and apologized with submissive eyes, head tilted toward her feet, after the most modest and quick connection with Harvey's eyes.

"You need help carrying that, Lena!"

"No sir. I have it." Lena turned to proceed through the living room. She thought Harvey was pleasant enough. She had been careful not to let anyone see her during the seconds that she looked at his face and his body the previous few times that they needed to be in the same space at the same time. She noticed that he was handsome, well-built, but seemed to neglect his hygiene. She could smell his perspiration.

Harvey insisted on helping Lena. He blocked her way and

took the basket of clothes from her hands, and in so doing, pushed her backward. Lena had learned to laugh softly when encountering the aggression of men. It was an attempt to disarm them. Harvey nudged her again with the basket. Lena uncharacteristically looked directly into his face.

There was wildness about his bright eyes and laughing mouth. He nudged again, and then dropped the basket, spilling the contents onto the living room floor. As Lena leaned to refill the basket, Harvey grasped her arms and shoved her small frame onto the sofa.

Embarrassed, she tried to stand but Harvey blocked her. He pushed his face down to her and whispered, "You're pretty, Lena." The image of Sarah in the bedroom two doors away from them filled Lena's mind. She felt the slickness of the sweat and oil on Harvey's face against her own face. She also felt his whiskers and the softness of his skin. He smelled like a thing stored away in a dark place for years. They struggled, both careful not to make a noise, each for their own reasons. Lena resisted but simultaneously believed that she was wrong to do so. She knew that she could not win.

Through a knotted emptiness in her stomach and sharp thoughts of her father's aggressions toward her, Lena registered Harvey tugging at her underwear. Before she could further resist, the fronts of her own thighs were pressed against her skirt that lay tumbled in a bunch upon her chest. Within seconds, Harvey grunted his semen into her.

As quietly as he had approached her, Harvey left. For the ten remaining days until Sarah was back on her feet, Harvey repeated the act with Lena multiple times. Each time afterwards, Harvey turned his back to Lena, went to Sarah's room, and kneeled beside her bed to pray a prayer for her health and another asking God and Sarah to forgive him for being a mortal man tainted by original sin.

Lena found comfort in both the quickness of Harvey's act and his prayers. She whispered her own prayers each time as she rearranged her clothing on her body.

By the final encounter, Lena no longer resisted Harvey. Given the choice that she did not have, she preferred him to working under her father's brutal gaze. Lena believed that Harvey thought her a special person. She imagined that Harvey might prefer her if Sarah died. This trouble produced my mother, Ovella, Lena's first child.

∞

In Star, forty miles southeast of where my mother, Ovella, was conceived, my father, Rob Gaddy, lived and worked on the Allen farm. He was already eighteen when his future wife, Ovella, was born.

∞

Rob had commenced his adult life in the summer of 1923, when he was eleven years old. He left his parents' Morven, North Carolina home after his father, Christopher Gaddy, a colored farmer descended from emancipated slaves, died of a stroke in the wheat field of their thirty-seven-acre farm.

Following my grandfather Christopher's death, his English-Cherokee wife, the former Idella Grooms, took stock of her situation. The two had been an interracial couple married several decades after the Civil War, before anti-interracial marriage laws were reconstructed in the South.

The widow Idella, her son (my father, Rob), and three of my father's ten siblings were left to tend their farm during one of the South's many agricultural depressions. Rather than continue on the near impossible course set by Christopher, Idella decided to sell the house, barns and land. She would move to the city, to Durham where her daughter, Janie, already lived. Janie's husband, Frank, was employed in the thriving tobacco processing industry there.

Idella's decision to sell the farm left eleven-year-old Rob at the first major crossroads of his young life. On the sixth morning after his father's death, Rob, the darkest complexioned of Idella and Christopher's racially blended children, announced from the farmhouse porch where he stood with his mother, two older sisters and younger brother, "Ma I'm gonna go out and make a living for myself." Rob's little brother Will, only five at the time, pulled at his big brother's pant leg and echoed, "I'm going to make a living, Mama."

While he and his mother looked out over a battered garden of dewberries, asparagus, tomatoes and corn damaged from a June hail storm the prior evening and onto the wheat field beyond, Idella with glassy eyes still directed toward the crops said to her son, "Go on then, Rob. I wish you the best." With eyelids half closed and eyes focused on the black soil of the front yard, she added in a softer tone, "Lord knows I don't know how I'm gonna keep food in all your bellies."

The same morning, Rob left the home where he had spent his entire life. Armed with a clean rag that held three fried fatback biscuit sandwiches and the assurance of a man, he walked out of the yard past the garden, then past the wheat field in the direction of the closest large town. Wadesboro was some nine miles away. He expected to reach the town by late evening if he did not tarry by the creek where he and his siblings caught crawfish nor rest too long under oak trees allowing his sweaty brow to dry.

Hours into his journey, while he contemplated a new life where he would stand tall and alone, where he would milk cows, pitch forks full of hay into a horse's feed trough and plow a field the same as his father had, the rhythmic clip-clop of a horse-drawn buggy interrupted his thoughts.

A white man sitting beside a woman of the same complexion pulled up by him. "Where you headed, Sonny?" The man's eyes were crossed. One eye looked straight at Rob while the other seemed to look elsewhere.

"I'm going off to make a living for myself, sir."

"Is that a fact?" The man paused to think as he looked Rob over. "Well then, we're looking for a farm hand over at our place in Star."

Without further discussion and only a vague knowledge of where Star might be, Rob climbed onto the back of the man's buggy. "My daddy just died. Buried him six days ago. I told my mama I was going off to make a living for myself and she thought it was a good idea. Ma's gonna sell our farm and move to Durham."

"You not going with her?"

"No sir. Got no use for a city."

As Rob spilled on about his family and the only life he had ever known–farm life—Barney Allen turned the buggy back toward Morven. "We better be askin' your mama first, if you can work for us."

Barney and Mary Allen gained permission to employ Rob at the rate of room and board plus fifty cents a week. Seven years passed before Rob saw his mother and siblings again.

∞

Seven years also passed before Rob's wife-to-be (my mother) was born. In the summer of 1931, when Ovella came into the world, Rob was eighteen. His daily life on the Allen farm involved rising before dawn to tend the animals and crops. Since he had arrived at the Allens at age eleven, Rob had joined them for their regular weekend activity of swigging *white lightning* liquor. By the time Ovella and Rob's destinies crossed, he had twenty-five years of drinking experience over her.

2

The first time Rob saw Ovella, he was transfixed, caught off guard. She stood on her Aunt Annie's porch in an olive green dress that hugged her waist. Her hair hung loose to her shoulders and she had the most exotic-looking face he had ever seen. She reminded him of the photographs of the film star Dorothy Lamour. In his characteristically friendly, outgoing and fun-loving way, Rob began a conversation with the young woman in the presence of Annie, who was single and closer to his age than was Ovella.

"Well hey there. How you today?" Rob tipped his head and removed his Stetson-style hat.

Ovella thought Rob to be handsome enough. He was tall, husky, with medium brown skin that had a transparency about it that gave the illusion that you might be able to see through to the man inside. But, due to the age difference, accentuated by his premature balding, she was not initially attracted to him. "I'm just fine." She shifted her weight from one foot to the other and propped a hand on her waist. Annie smiled.

"Rob, this is my niece. She lives with me when she's not working for Dr. Cranford over in Asheboro."

"The Cranfords? What you do for them?"

"I'm their nanny."

"You know, I've worked for them myself. Yard work a time or two."

With the Cranfords in common, Ovella perked up and engaged in an interchange about the doctor, about Asheboro, and Montgomery County where Rob lived and worked. Finally they talked about Liberty where she was born and raised.

By the time my parents met in 1950, my mother had grown into an outgoing and responsible nineteen-year-old woman. She had a standard mulatto look, a look not shared by her siblings as they were all biological products of their *colored* parents, Kiah and Lena. Ovella had creamy white skin, tinged with the slightest gold, more closely resembling her English biological parent, Harvey. She had long black hair, straight compared to her siblings' hair but curly compared to that of most white people. Her eyes were a rich brown. Her frame was small.

As a live-in nanny for the Cranfords, Ovella earned room and board plus three dollars per week for caring for their two children, a girl and a boy. She had lived with her Aunt Annie, in a small town just outside of Asheboro since she was sixteen, after Kiah, the father who raised her, died and left Lena unable to provide for Ovella and her seven younger siblings.

When my father and mother met on the back porch of Aunt Annie's two-story former farm house, surrounded by a few dilapidated barns and an abundance of weeds, Rob had already lived double her years. He was the supplier of the homemade brand of liquor–*white lightning*–that Annie sold by the drink to customers from miles around.

Rob had begun to run liquor thirteen years earlier, after he stopped sharecropping on the Allens' farm. Since age twenty-five, he had worked as a cook and a liquor runner for the owner of a Candor, North Carolina diner.

My father returned to Aunt Annie's more often after he met my mother and even showed up at the Cranfords asking if they needed yard work. Eventually the two began taking Sunday drives to Candor, where Rob worked at the diner, and to Biscoe, where there was a juke joint that they enjoyed together with local black folks.

But it was at Annie's house where Rob introduced Ovella to drinking shots of liquor. She had had the occasional beer and liked the taste, but a shot of hard liquor was a new experience.

"Pour Ovella one too, Annie. This batch is good. Take a look at how clear it is." Annie took in her niece's somber expression.

"You want one?"

"I'll try it."

That is where it began. The warmth of the homemade eighty proof white lightning liquor going down Ovella's throat burned, warmed her sinuses, made her eyes tear, and filled her from the inside out as nothing had ever before. She took a slow deep breath and felt a freshness and clearness in her head. "Whooh! That's strong!" Annie, Rob and Ovella laughed together.

"Give her another one."

"Oh no. One's enough." Ovella said the words but thought, *I can't wait to have another one.* She didn't want to appear greedy or unladylike. She promised herself that she would have another as soon as the right amount of time passed. The right amount of time was close to thirty minutes. She reveled in the feelings of confidence, increased maturity and sensuality that came along with the drink. She did not have a clue at the time where those first two shots would lead.

In the fall of 1951, a year after meeting, Rob and Ovella married. They had their first child a year after their small justice-of-the-peace wedding. They named their son Robert Gaddy Jr., and called him Lee.

Years later, when my father was not present, my mother would say, "Rob was older and more experienced than me. He knew how to get his way." She shared these words with a far-away look in her eyes, a look that seemed to transport her to another time, a look that seemed to encompass potential and regret in the same space. The message, intended or not, became coupled in my mind with a lesson about watching out for older men. But as a child, all I knew of men was through my father. His older man faults were not distinguishable to my eyes.

∞

My mother told me many times over the course of my life with her that she was complete when I was born two years after my brother. Her dream had been to marry and have two children—a boy and a girl, in that order. By the age of twenty-three, her dream was fulfilled with my birth. I, the second child, the first daughter, completed the picture of a perfect family for my mother.

But by the time my first birthday arrived, my family was homeless and my parents apart. My father, at forty-two years old, was in the hospital being diagnosed with chronic alcoholism and early stages of liver cirrhosis and my mother, brother and I were back at Aunt Annie's.

My mother, on my first birthday, sat in the living room of her aunt's rural home with the two children who had made her life perfect, most likely thinking of Daddy. He, was lying in a bed at Duke Medical Center in Durham, most likely trying to figure out why his lips, arms, hands and legs were numb. He told the doctors "I can't walk right." For ten months his limbs and lips had been in varied states of dysfunction. He thought he was either dying or going crippled. It turned out to be poisoning from the white lightning liquor he'd been drinking.

Even though Daddy told the doctors "I didn't start drinking 'til *after* my legs went numb," they figured better. He told them, "I had to quit my job four months ago 'cause I was unsteady on the ladder." (He had since Lee's birth, stopped running liquor and took employment with the younger Allen son's construction company.)

The truth was, though, that before his hospitalization, the father whose lap I loved sitting in had been drinking a pint of liquor daily. What a sorrow-filled day it was for me, as an adult, to learn that during the first year of my life, while

I was getting acquainted with this world, Daddy was drinking his way into a hospital.

The doctors sent my father home after a week, with vitamins for beriberi and the directive to avoid the alcohol. They didn't know much about helping alcoholics in 1955. Alcoholics Anonymous was only a speck on the American radar and didn't exist at all in the rural South at that time. Being an illiterate dark-skinned man without money gave Daddy fewer options than an alcoholic with money would have had. Even if the doctors had recommended a rest away from the demands of life in a drying-out spa somewhere, there would have been no way for my father to take the treatment.

The doctors ignored my father's symptoms of depression and anxiety that were observed and written into the medical record during the two-month course that included hospitalization and follow-up appointments. Mental illness was a stigma as misunderstood as alcoholism at the time, and treatment was as far out of reach for my father as for alcoholism.

∞

A few months after Daddy's hospitalization, after he regained steadiness on his feet, he and my mother took their perfect little family from Aunt Annie's to their new home. We moved to the smallest town in Montgomery County, to Star, back to where my father had spent half of his childhood and his early adult years. Our first house in Star was on the Allens' homestead where Daddy had worked for fifteen years, first as a farm hand and later as a sharecropper.

The white people that my father had worked for from the time he was a child of eleven years old welcomed him and his new family home.

3

Star, North Carolina was a town of seven hundred people in 1955. Over ninety five percent of its population was Caucasian. The remainder black people, mostly with the last names of Green or Dunn, thus calling the colored section, Dunn-Green Town.

Star, like many small southern villages, had a downtown area consisting of a grocery store, a small department store, a post office, a drug store, a gas station and a boarding house. North of the town was its hosiery mill. The citizens living nearest downtown were white. Dunn-Green Town was farther away, on the other side of the railroad tracks to the south.

The Allens lived on the opposite side of town from the Dunn-Green community in a rural part of Star. Though I was only one and Lee three when we arrived in Star in the late fall of 1955, I flourished in the place where my parents, my brother and I began to be the family that my mother had intended. I grew into our home and the land of the Allens' homestead, the place where my father had spent half his childhood and his early adult years.

Though the animals and crops were gone because the

place was no longer an operating farm, Rob Gaddy had the chance to tend his family, to appreciate with clear eyes and mind the growth in his children, the same as he had appreciated the growth o the gardens, the chicks, and the calves of the past.

From the grayed wood-framed house that sat more than eight hundred yards across the asphalt road from Mary and Barney Allen's painted green-shuttered house, our father recounted his days tilling the Allens' fields that he later sharecropped with them. He told us of fishing in the pond behind the house and of squirting warm milk at dawn from the cow's teats.

But when he was on his own, he may have recalled an eleven-year-old boy being soothed by the *white lightning* that first year with the Allens. The liquor helped him sleep when his thoughts were too active. The sharp clear elixir calmed his nerves, gave him courage and lessened the loneliness that always threatened to assault him at bedtime. He was haunted by memories of days on the farm when he slept alone without the noise of his sisters, brother, father and mother. Alcohol might have been the closest the boy could come to feeling something like the comfort of two strong arms wrapped around him, where there were not any.

At first, after returning to the Allens' place, Rob believed that the alcohol was something he needed to leave behind. He was glad for a home and a fresh start with his family. But the same home reminded him of his closest friend, the bottle. Before very long, alcohol returned as his companion and continued on its journey of eroding his vital organs.

∞

It was the cold winter of 1957 and 1958 that gave me memory of my English-Cherokee Grandma Idella. I was three and a half years old and had made too much noise. My father's mother had come to live with us in the house on the Allens' homestead because she was sick and my mother could look after her.

The hard plastic doll crashed for the third time onto the wood floor that shined from years of people walking on it. "If you drop that doll again, I'm going to throw this glass of water right through you!" The old woman in the bed had long white and brown hair that blanketed her shoulders. The doll that I held was almost as big as me, which made it hard to grip. Maybe if I had not been sitting so high in a straight-backed chair, I would have been able to hold the doll better. I became afraid to move.

My mother and father told people that I was the spitting image of this old woman, my father's mother. At the time, I didn't know how a young child could be the spitting image of someone so old. Noticing the fear and sadness on my face as I sat across from Grandma's bed, Mama said, "Grandma 'Della loves you." Although my mother reminded me of my grandmother's love many times in the years to come, I only remembered that she was once so mad at me that she threatened to throw a glass of water through me.

∞

The winter day in January 1958 when Grandma Idella died was a black day. According to Cherokee belief, it was the moon segment, the western direction of This World, the

27

world between the perfectly ordered and predictable upper world and the disordered and unstable lower world. Black was the color assigned to the West and it stood for the region of the souls of the dead and for death itself.

After Grandma Idella died, all kinds of people came around dressed in black clothes. They brought food on plates, in pots and in bowls. Everyone seemed serious and they all talked at the same time.

Weepy women who called themselves 'aunts' said that I was very pretty. They said that I had their mother's wavy brown hair, her green eyes and her fair complexion. They looked at me in a dreamy kind of way. They touched my hair and said "Darling, your hair is so soft." I felt glad to favor Grandma Idella because it made the aunts love me. They held me in their laps and patted me with their warm, per-fumed hands.

Daddy said that a woman's hair was her glory. The aunts said the same thing. "A woman's hair is her glory." All the aunts agreed. "She must never cut it. No, never." I looked at my Aunt Peg's hair, in whose lap I was sitting and tried to see the glory in it. I touched my own hair. I could not for the life of me make out which part of the hair was glory, but I did know that my hair was special because it was like Grandma Idella's and because the aunts and Daddy said that she had beautiful hair.

∞

The aunts reminded my father of Grandma Idella's Cherokee belief about death, specifically that her soul was lingering around our house, and would continue for as long as she had been staying there with us. Her soul's next stop would be Aunt Janie's house in Durham to linger for as long as she had lived there, which was a long time. "How long was she in Durham?" the oldest sister, Aunt Jessie, asked and then answered in her slow melodic southern drawl. "Let's see now. She went up to Janie's in 1923." The other aunts nodded their heads in agreement. "And it's 1958 now. That's how long?"

I looked at the ceiling and into the corners of the room for Grandma's soul while everybody did math in their heads and on their fingers. The smoke from Mama's Salems, Aunt Peg's cigarette and Daddy's L&Ms wafted through the air and around the grown-ups like ghosts trying to get free. The smoke smell clung to their hair and clothes. I examined the smoke and the corners of the ceiling for Grandma's soul. I rubbed the sting in my nose. I could not tell the smoke from a soul.

Before the rest of the aunts could finish calculating the number of years that my grandmother lived in Durham, Aunt Jessie concluded, "It was 35 years." Everyone shook their heads in wonderment. Daddy looked at the floor with one hand shoved in the pocket of the dark gray trousers that he had not worn since some other family member had died and brought people together.

After talking about Grandma Idella's soul, the aunts, who were all older and lighter complexioned than my father, talked about the racial tension rising in their cities; in Greensboro and Durham, North Carolina, and Plainfield, New Jersey. Daddy remained in the doorway between the

29

kitchen and the living room where the four aunts and my mother sat. I settled into Aunt Peg's lap. With cigarette smoke floating around my aunt's face, she spoke the transformed diction of southerners who migrated northward. "I for one say that it's time for black people to get an equal education to whites."

Aunt Jessie, the oldest of the sisters, added, "Well sir! That might be right. But we goin' to have a lot more sad days 'tween here and there."

Aunt Janie was the darkest complexioned of the four sisters. She held a dip of snuff between her lower lip and gum. Her voice hummed when she spoke. "Seems to me they forcing things on everybody, colored and white. In Durham, folks got no trouble with the colored schools."

I fanned my face as Aunt Peg removed the half smoked cigarette from between her lips and spoke emphatically. "Now you know that black children in the South are getting the whites' used books and used furniture. And the black teachers don't get paid anywhere near what the white ones get." The aunts listened while the cigarette smoke swirled around Aunt Peg's eyes, causing her to squint and fan herself with her free hand. "The only way black folks are going to make it, is through education. It's the only way!"

"May be," Aunt Julia, who had not said a thing, interjected. My mother and father held each other's gaze.

Aunt Peg continued. "All this prejudice is what made me leave North Carolina and go to Jersey in the first place." She replaced the cigarette between her lips and took a long pull, making the cigarette crackle like burning wood in a wood stove.

Daddy continued listening to his older sisters as Aunt Jessie added, "All I can say is that Mama must be glad to've left this crazy business behind her."

Aunt Janie chuckled. "Don't make no kinda sense!" Then she sobered. "That colored child in Little Rock, Arkansas had to have soldiers take her to that white school."

Aunt Peg chuckled. "The whites scared their children gonna catch some black from the colored children."

All of the aunts laughed but my father and mother did not. Not one of the aunts had a child young enough to be affected by desegregation directly.

∞

Months after Grandma Idella was buried, when spring was breaking, Mary Allen announced to me and my five and a half year old brother Lee, "Me and Barney raised your daddy." Lee and I stopped playing to listen to Mamu, as we had come to call the small, bespectacled white woman. "He came to live with us when he was just a boy. He was always a hard worker. We took care of him like one of our own."

What Mary Allen didn't say that day was that they gave our father room, board and some change every week, when they had it, for his labor on their farm. The Allen children–two boys both younger than my father—were sent to school. The children that Mary Allen gave birth to and raised learned how to read and write, unlike my father, who was illiterate. The younger of the two Allen sons owned and operated a construction company. That son, though fifteen years younger, employed my father.

Since the Allens thought of themselves as parents of a sort to my father (and even though Lee and I took after the white relatives in our colored family—having fair skin and wavy hair), they called us their "colored grandchildren." We were taught to call them by the same name as their real white grandchildren called them. So Lee and I, and later on my little brown-skinned younger brother Dale, addressed them as Mamu and Papa. The Allens' white grandchildren were several years older than my brothers and me. Not knowing any better or having been affected by the realities of the South's social order yet, I loved Mamu and Papa and I adored my white cousins.

Helen Allen, Mamu and Papa's one girl grandchild, was my first best friend. She was three years older than I and had long red hair, freckles, and creamy white skin. While her mother worked at Star's post office during the day, my mother took care of Helen. She was as much my world as my own family during the years between my first and fourth birthdays. Helen introduced me to sugar biscuits—my mother's cold biscuit sliced through the middle with white sugar sprinkled inside. She introduced me to softball games watched from the woods along the edge of the white kids' elementary school athletic field. We rolled ourselves in blankets and slithered across the floor like worms together. I happily wore the clothes that Helen outgrew.

But Brown versus the Board of Education had been settled and the repercussions by 1958 began seeping into the life of our little town. According to law, segregation of schools and other public facilities in the South was no longer an option. Papa Barney on one July Saturday morning, just before I turned four and as Lee was being prepared to go to first grade, said to my father, "We got the best colored people around right here in Star. They don't make trouble like some in other places. Everything was fine 'til they started up all this integration business. Got everybody all stirred up."

Daddy listened to Papa Barney but wondered out loud with my mother later, "Which school are we supposed to send Lee to?"

Mama thought for a few seconds. "Well, we live right around the corner from the white school. But look what it took to get those children in Little Rock into a white school."

"Ain't no way I'm gonna have a child of mine marched into the first grade with gun-carrying soldiers. If they don't want him there, ain't gonna force him on them."

"What did Barney say?"

"Don't think he likes the idea of integration."

"What?"

"He thinks it's stirring up trouble. Stirring up colored folks."

"No!" Mama's incredulous expression made Daddy mad.

"Well, who the hell wants trouble?" He walked away from my mother, holding inside the caring he had for his own non-African mother and the Allens, and a growing awareness that life should be better for darker-skinned people.

As the summer of 1958 progressed, the backlash from

forced desegregation was affecting my family. Having a so-called colored family, my own, living in the middle of a white southern town, playing with white children as though they could have real familial-type mingling became too self-conscious for everyone. It did not matter that both of my parents had a parent each of European descent, along with their parents of African descent. As far as anyone was concerned, we were Negros, over and done, nothing in between or other than. Even one drop of Negro blood made a person black. Segregation meant separate. Integration messed with the comfortable social order of people. The pressures to stand either with the whites or with the blacks on the issue shrank the space available for the folks who had chosen to live in the space between the two worlds – namely my family and the Allens.

Grandma's death, the alcohol that my father had again succumbed to, and then all the tension over integration seemed to change things between my parents. They began yelling at one another. They threw dishes. Plates and cups crashed and shattered against walls. My parents' lips moved fast and they glared at each other. Dale, who was a toddler in the summer of 1958, and I cried during their fights. Lee, at nearly six years old, had begun practicing the suppression of any emotion other than anger that my parents' aggression caused him. He stood in his little boy's body and told Dale and me with a frown on his face, "Stop crying! Be quiet!"

Mama scooped me into her arms, propped me on her hip and carried me outside. She picked up a rock and yelled into the house that Daddy better "Git" or she was going to hit him in the head with the rock. Daddy left. That summer morning in 1958, there in the comfort of my mother's arms, I had no idea that my mother's strength during a fight between my parents had numbered days. It wasn't long after one of my parents' Sunday morning fights that we moved from the Allens' homestead.

4

Before my fourth birthday, and before my older brother Lee started first grade, I had to say good-bye to Helen Allen, my best friend, and to my white grandparents. Since all the white folks including the Allens seemed to value segregation, separate blacks and whites, my daddy and Mama were forced to undo the integration that my family had been practicing for the previous three years. We moved from the Allens' homestead in the middle of the white part of Star to Biscoe, the next town to the west.

Our next home was beside a black family, the Goldstones. The houses that our two families occupied sat down a dirt road across the highway from the Biscoe drive-in. Along with a new place to live, I made a new friend my same age–Kathleen Goldstone, or *Red,* as her family called her because of her red hair. When I pressed Red's hair with my hand, it sprang right back into position like a wet sponge.

The two older Goldstone sisters, Ruth and Jean, already almost grown women, were always popping in when Daddy was at work, borrowing this thing or that of Mama's. "That sho' is a pretty dress Ovella. I'd look good in that on my wedding day." Jean wore my mother's deep purple satin dress to get married.

Ruth chose a pair of Mama's high heeled shoes for going out clubbing with her friends. Makeup, perfume, jewelry, everything Mama had from her days as an independent woman, they wanted. With three young children, one in diapers, and nothing to do but cook and clean, Mama easily lent her things out. But Daddy did not like it. Ruth and Jean brought liquor with them to our house. The visits and liquoring up interfered with dinner-time promptness, children's clean faces and tending to the laundry.

First Daddy told Mama, "I don't want them up here hanging 'round during the day. You tell them to go on back home when they come next time." Mama's response was to look at our father in a perturbed manner and puff on a cigarette. But before Mama could talk to Ruth and Jean, Daddy took his opportunity when they walked past our house. "How y'all?" He was polite at first. Then in a lower and more serious voice he said, "Ovella has things to do to take care of the house and the children. I don't want y'all bothering her during the day."

They exchanged a few more words and the sisters walked off without saying good-bye, releasing undecipherable noises born in their throats. Daddy forbade Lee and me from going into the Goldstones' home. "They steal," our father said. The prohibition did not much matter for they rarely invited us in. Needless to say, the forbidding caused a strain between our two households. Before long, when Ruth or Jean passed our house on foot, they sneered and cussed out loud, calling "Half-breeds" at whoever might be listening.

"What's a half-breed, Daddy?" I asked my father once after hearing their words.

"Nothing. They're jealous 'cause you're so pretty."

For the remainder of the summer that we lived next to the Goldstones, Red and her older brothers, James and William, played with Lee and me, nicely, in the sandy path between our houses. When school started, Lee walked with James and William to the end of the dirt road to catch the bus that took the black kids to Brutonville Elementary School in Candor.

For the first week of Lee's first year in school, Mama took me and Dale with her as she walked Lee, James and William to the bus stop. We watched the three boys climb the stairs of the large yellow bus already packed with kids and I waved to Lee as the bus drove off. I felt excited about someone in our family going off to learn to read books, to play with new friends on a playground at recess and to spend a day with a teacher. I also felt disconcerted. I was not used to having only myself and Dale to occupy my time for an entire day. I missed Lee and waited for him at the end of each school day.

∞

Early in the school year, trouble broke out between Lee and the Goldstone boys. They scuffled on the walk home from the bus stop one day. Lee said that the brothers teamed up on him and called him that name that I thought had to do with jealousy—half-breed. The injustice of older and bigger boys whipping on Lee caused me distress. Mama began

39

walking me and Dale to the bus stop at the end of the day to meet Lee so as to prevent fights. James and William ran home ahead of us while Mama inquired about Lee's day.

∞

When winter cold arrived, air leaked into our house from the holes and cracks in our walls and floors. I watched my father make rounds from tree trunks into firewood for heating and cooking. He raised the ax high above his head then slammed it into the wood perched upon a chopping block. The resulting halves were placed on the block again and split smaller still. With each swing, Daddy grunted and expelled breath out of his body like a squeezed bag. The pine and oak smells from the logs filled the air. My father stopped to cough phlegm from his lungs into his mouth to spit out. He had bad sinuses that produced copious fluid and caused bad headaches if it wasn't expelled—so he either, with thumb held against a nostril, blew it out of his nose into the air, or discharged it into one of his blue bandana handkerchiefs.

One winter evening between Daddy's coming home from his job at J. F. Allen's construction company and Mama's dinner of cabbage, pork chops, rice and hot biscuits, our father stood in the window admiring the large pile of wood that he had split. "We'll be warm this winter," he repeated several times.

We took our seats around the dining table but before our first bite of food, Daddy jumped up and went back to the kitchen window. "Damn it to hell!" spilled out his mouth.

He moved quicker than I usually saw him move and rushed outside. My mother, Lee and I ran to the window.

"What the hell y'all doing? Bring that wood back here now!" Daddy yelled from beside the woodpile. Beyond him, running down the path to the Goldstone's were James and William carrying some of our wood in their arms. Daddy took off after them. I did not recall having seen my father run before. It did not look like a natural state of movement for him.

Mama said, "Uh oh," and took a Salem cigarette from its green and white pack. I watched as Daddy became smaller in the distance. We saw Mr. Goldstone step out of his house and the next thing you knew, he and my father were jerking their arms around in the air and talking loudly. Daddy soon returned with the armful of wood.

∞

The same night as the Goldstone boys tried to make off with our wood, a snowstorm rolled in while everyone slept. Daddy went to work as usual the next morning driving the Allens' red pick-up truck. Lee did not go to school as the slippery roads prevented school buses from traveling.

The exuberance caused by the snow allowed Mrs. Goldstone and Mama to forget about the tensions between us for a while. Red, James, William, Lee and I threw snowballs and built snow men along the path between our house and theirs. Lee, Red, and I watched James and William make a trap for birds. They propped a board up on one end with a stick. A string was tied to the stick and was held on to from behind a tree. As soon as a bird went under the plank and

41

pecked at bread crumbs, a snatch of the string brought the board down.

Without my father or Mr. Goldstone at home, Lee and I followed Red, James and William to their house where we watched Mrs. Goldstone dunk the birds into a pan of boiling hot water before plucking off the feathers. She then slid the birds onto a stick to be cooked over the fire in the wood stove like a hotdog. At the same moment as I began fearing that I would be offered some of the bird to eat, Lee motioned to me to go.

As we were leaving, Mrs. Goldstone announced that somebody should go out and get some wood. This brought back images of the previous night and I feared a reoccurrence of the wood theft without our father at home to act as guard. I was amazed to see James go straight to the side of their house and pull boards off. I told Mama about this approach to gathering firewood and she shook her head in amazement. At the young age of four and a half, even I could figure out that burning the boards that made your house would result in the house's disappearance and then where would you be for keeping warm?

When I told Mama about the bird eating, after she was over being mad about us being in the Goldstone's house, she said, "Ain't enough meat on those birds for nothing."

∞

When spring broke, eight months after we moved in beside the Goldstone's, we moved again. The new place was back in Star but over a mile from white people and more than three miles from blacks. At the new place, Daddy gathered me and Lee together in the backyard and as he sat on an oak tree stump, he drew on a piece of cardboard with the stubby pencil he carried in his bib overalls pocket. He raised the cardboard and pointed to primitive-looking figures. "These are the Goldstone's. They're monkeys." Daddy gave each monkey one of the Goldstone's names. "That's Jean. That's Ruth. This one is William." And so on.

I do not recall another time when my father spoke derogatorily about other people. It was also the first and last time I saw him express himself with a pencil or pen on a writing surface. I was struck by the fact that Daddy thought the Goldstones to be less than us.

∞

Our new home was free of neighbors for miles. To look at the property that we rented down in the woods of Star, one might have thought it a trashy sight. The Allens' old red truck sat out front of a grayed wood house. Piles of rusted tin cans that once held green beans, corn or beets were piled high in mounds around the yard. There were the clearings in the surrounding fields where my family and I would either go to the toilet on the ground or empty our night chambers.

But I, a curious four and a half year old, saw the place as nothing less than our castle with porches on the front and back, a big cedar tree twice as tall as the house to the side and the surrounding woods extending for miles in all directions. The once-loved-then-abandoned former tobacco homestead seemed the best place on earth to me.

The house itself had four rooms – two bedrooms, a

kitchen and, what seemed to my eyes, a very large living room. My parents decided to use the living room as a bedroom for all five of us to sleep. One bed for my parents and another bed for me and my two brothers. An unused bed sat coverless in a corner of the bedroom. "It won't take as much fire wood to heat the smaller rooms. The bedroom doesn't need heat," Daddy explained to Mama. My parents stationed our dining table in one of the former bedroom spaces next to the kitchen. The heat from the wood stove would keep that room warm. The second former bedroom served as a cozy living room with its own fireplace.

On the property was a well that Daddy said would never run dry. Plots of land to the east of the house had been gardens. Remnants of corn stalks were strewn about it. Edibles around the property included a mature persimmon tree, a muscadine grape vine, blackberry patches, wild rabbits prime for trapping, a possum here and there, and white-tailed deer. Wild varieties of vegetables included creasy greens and polk salad, which augmented store-bought staples of flour, rice and grits, lard, fish, meats, dried pinto beans and black eyed peas.

Daddy told us that the homestead had once thrived. "See those buildings? Those are tobacco barns." He pointed to the terraced hills east of the house and then to a large field. "That's where they grew the tobacco." My father further identified mature apple trees beginning to bud leaves, and the garden area where tomatoes, beans, corn, and cucumbers were raised to eat fresh or to can.

"Come over here." We followed Daddy to the round

structure with the wooden lid. A rope and tin bucket dangled from a wooden frame. Daddy removed the lid from over a hollow-sounding hole and lowered the bucket down into the well. "Nobody but Lee, your mama and me can draw water from this well. You hear?" Daddy looked at all of us. As he turned the metal handle that lowered the bucket he said, "This handle can fly back and knock you smack in the head or bust out your teeth." I covered my mouth. An image of my teeth cracked and bleeding was all I needed to stay clear of the handle.

My father spoke further as he looked out over the property. "When this was a farm, the children had to get up before the sun rose and help milk the cow, feed the hogs and chickens and gather eggs." We watched and listened to Daddy talk. The wooden frame over the well squeaked as he drew the filled bucket out of the well.

The spring day was warm and sunny. The well water was cold and sweet. Daddy explained that the old homestead life was how his family lived when he was growing up. "Everything was over after my daddy died. The Agricultural Depression was on us. Farmers went to work in tobacco plants and cotton mills."

"Are we gonna make a farm Daddy?" I asked.

"We can have some chickens and a garden."

I was excited by the prospects. The surrounding woods, the dilapidated barns, the terraced hills called to me as strongly as anything I had known in my entire life. I could not have been happier.

∞

I was five when we took possession of our first television. It was the winter of 1959. Piedmont North Carolina was having its usual mild winter. My father didn't need to wear a jacket when he went outside. His white t-shirt under bib overalls was what he wore on the day he installed the antenna for our used black and white Zenith.

My mother and father, seven-year-old Lee, three-year-old Dale and I encircled the television. We were enthralled by the vague images of people flickering through what came to be known to us as *snow*.

Our father had placed a ladder against the house. He had stuck the base of the antenna pole into the hole he had dug. The antenna leaned against the house. He left us and went outside to climb the ladder and connect the antenna to the frame of the house with thick wire. The magic of a clear picture would happen by connecting a flat brown wire that ran from our television out a window to the antenna.

My mother, my brothers and I waited for clarity to appear on the screen. Lee decided he would break from the *snow* and check on our father. The wooden door slammed shut behind him. Dale traveled about the living room banging on various things with a stick. "Come look at the picture," Mama coaxed him.

Then there was a series of bumps on the outside wall of the house. The picture on the television screen surged into deeper snow. My mother and I turned our heads toward where we heard the sound. Lee flung the door open behind us.

"Mama, Ma. Daddy fell. He's bleeding!"

46

My mother spun around and raced out of the house, leaving the door standing open for the cool air to enter. As I reached the door in front of Dale, I saw my father, his right arm extended out from his body. He climbed the steps onto the front porch. I grabbed Dale and pulled him back.

Mama yelled for me to, "Get back. Get out of the way." She ran ahead of my father. Lee trailed behind them. My mother rushed past me saying again, "Get back. Get Dale out of the way."

As I pulled my resisting little brother back into the room, I did not take my eyes from my father and his out-swung arm. I gasped as I registered the deep apple-red blossom formed on his white t-shirt at his armpit. I held a squirming Dale firmly.

My mother returned and ordered my father to sit on the sofa. She carried a bath towel. She examined the bloody area that grew in size and wetness. "You've cut the artery," she said. "You have to go the doctor."

My father sat still and dazed as my mother tugged and wrapped a towel against his underarm and over his shoulder twice. As Mama wrapped, she explained to Lee that he was to take good care of me and Dale while she took Daddy uptown to see Dr. Scarborough. That day my three- and seven-year-old brothers and I, at five years of age, were left at home alone for the first time in my memory. Lee stood tall and said, "I'll watch them." He looked at Dale and me with confident eyes. Though my parents were back within hours, my father's cut stitched, I would embrace and reject the confused and conflicted feelings of being parentless a thousand times in my life to come.

5

Lee and I ran ahead. Three-year-old Dale rambled behind us barely able to keep pace. I looked back at my brothers. Lee and I laughed at Dale who worked extra hard to make the distances we made easily.

Sticks cracked and snapped beneath our feet. Tree branches flew back at Dale but did not deter him from moving forward. He had learned not to whine with us because we did not have sympathy for him. We did not care that he was two years younger than me or four years younger than Lee.

We ran fast and hard toward the creek. Brown leaves covered the entire floor of the forest and crunched as we ran. The leaves made our footsteps sound bigger than they were. The thumping sound came to my ears through my body. Sun shone in through the leafless trees. The sun and our sweat kept us warm in our fall clothes of long pants and long-sleeved shirts.

Twigs tangled in my hair. I did not care. All I wanted was to get to the creek. We were like wild animals lobbing through the woods. We ran downhill. Lee yelled, "Watch out for snakes." Dale and I squealed with delight and terror. We never saw snakes when we were in the woods playing.

The three of us arrived at the creek's bank. My cheeks tingled and felt hot to my cold hands. My face thumped with my heartbeat. Lee's face was red from running. Dale breathed hard. He was the happiest to see the water, flowing as fast as we had been running. I squatted down and dipped my hand into the water. It was ice cold. I felt thirsty and caught water in the cup of my two hands. I drank quickly before my hands numbed. I told Dale to drink too. He squatted and did as I said. My stomach felt full from the water and the smell of wet leaves.

We explored the creek using sticks to poke the bottom. Lee pointed to little fish– minnows–in the water racing from one place to the next. He touched a place in the mud on the bottom and a crawfish pushed further away from us to the under hang of the bank.

A log had fallen over the creek. "We can cross here," Lee shouted.

"You first," I told him.

"This is how you do it." Lee showed us how to walk on the log with arms extended out for balance. "Walk fast."

He crossed. I was next. The creek seemed far below us and wide. I crossed and then it was Dale's turn. Lee and I waited for him. He looked at the log. His face looked concerned. We urged, "Come on Dale. You can do it. Just step up and cross over." Dale climbed onto the log and crawled cautiously. Midway, he slipped and with a splash was on the creek bottom in water to his waist. "Get out." Lee and

I yelled. We knew that the water could make him cold fast. "Hurry up." We laughed. It was funny to see our little brother splashing in the cold water, teeth already chattering. "Hurry up." We chided him that a water moccasin might get him to make him move faster. He pulled himself onto the bank. His shoes squished from the water inside. He looked at us. Mad. He shook and flicked himself. His teeth chattered more violently.

"We better get him home," Lee said. I was disappointed. *This brother is always spoiling our fun* I thought. We headed home but not as fast as we came, because we had to walk uphill for a while.

Dale whined. "I'm cold."

Lee told him, "You better not cry or I'll give you something to cry about." Dale quieted and walked harder.

"You should be used to being wet from peeing in bed at night, Dale," I said.

Lee agreed and together we called "Peebag." Dale worked harder to climb the hill.

At home Daddy chopped wood and didn't pay us any attention. Inside Mama wanted to know why we let our little brother fall into the creek. "We couldn't help it," I said. She acted mad and kind of clumsy as she changed him into dry clothes.

For the rest of the day, Dale had to stay inside because his shoes were wet and without them he could not play outside. This was fine with me because I always had the most fun when it was just me and Lee–not little brother tagging on behind us holding us back. Lee and I were off again, leaving Dale where he belonged.

We climbed the terraced hills to the east of our house. We each climbed a pine tree that overlooked our house. We sat perched on limbs, hidden by the branches of the trees from our mother's, our father's and Dale's view. I laughed with delight as Dale's cries from the porch reached us, then sailed right on past and bounced back again in an echo. "Y'all come play with me."

∞

"Get up. Get your clothes on." Daddy rose early on Saturdays, the same as he did during the work week. He wanted everyone else up with him. His work boots sounded out the heaviness of his body as he walked into the bedroom. "Time to get up." The announcement was meant for my brothers, me and my mother. Lee and Dale stretched. Mama turned in the bed. My father paid no regard to what kind of hell he raised the night before and how late he had kept us up. Lee, Dale and I dragged ourselves out of the warm bed that we shared. "Get dressed. Put on some clothes," Daddy commanded. My brothers and I increased our pace and dressed.

That particular Saturday morning, Mama's slow dressing set Daddy off. While still in her nylon night gown and polyester bath robe, Mama placed breakfast before each of us at the table. Grits in a bowl with a melted-margarine pool on the surface, sugar and Pet evaporated canned milk added for extra flavor. I tried to enjoy the creamy smooth warmth of the cereal and ignore my father's harassment of my mother. "When you going to get some clothes on, Woman?" My mother's tactic had become to just remain quiet in the face of my father's demands. She set down a plate of fried eggs. My father scrubbed his work-booted feet back and forth beneath the table. "Why don't you put the damn eggs straight on my plate?" Mama snatched up the plate of fried eggs and slid two onto my father's plate.

After breakfast, my brothers and I went outside to play. The cool air felt good against my face which was over-heated from the combination of hot cereal, the heat of the wood stove, and long-sleeved pants and shirt. The fragrance of sun-warmed decomposing leaves filled my nose and lungs.

Piles of emptied liquor bottles and fruit jars accumulated at the rear of our house around the edge of the grassless yard. The *white lightning* type of liquor made down in the woods behind somebody's house came in a fruit jar. The bottle of liquor with a label came from an Alcoholic Beverage Commission or ABC store. The piles of bottles and jars had grown since we moved into our house several months earlier in the spring of the year.

"Pick some up." Lee directed Dale and me to gather the ABC store-bought bottles and carry them into the field. We left the fruit jars that were used in our bedroom at night for our family to pee into. "Put them there." Lee had Dale and me place standing bottles in a row on the ground. "Move back," he commanded us. "Get some rocks. Big ones." Dale and I gathered rocks, then stood beside Lee until he gave the direction, "Throw."

While we broke bottles, Mama readied herself to go to the

nearest neighbor's house to iron their laundry. My mother's calls from the back porch drew us home again. "We'll be a couple of hours. Lee you take care of your sister and brother. Don't go off into the woods, you hear?"

"Yes ma'am." Lee directed Dale and me into the living room where we piled in front of the Zenith for Saturday morning *Sunrise Theatre* and cartoons. I did not hear the sound of our parents leaving in the pickup truck.

We sat wherever we liked on those Saturday mornings when our parents were gone. On the back of the couch, on the arm of the couch, on the floor if we wished. Half way through television watching, I rose from my position and headed for our bedroom.

"Where you going?" Lee asked.

"To the bedroom."

"What for?"

Irritated with my brother for asking I replied, "To change my clothes."

"What are you going to change your clothes for?"

"Just because," I said and quickened my step away from his voice and into the room where my family slept. I closed the door behind me. Lee, distracted by *Night of the Living Dead*, relinquished his line of questioning.

Two unmade beds, one made bed with a heap of clothes from the clothes line piled on top, and the large bureau dresser with a mirror. I thought about climbing upon the bureau to look at the boxes of family pictures stacked on its shelves. But I was drawn to my parent's chest of drawers more strongly.

The bottom drawer was easiest to open because of my height and its proximity to the floor. The drawer contained several sets of cotton pajamas and maroon t-shirts that my father never wore, wrinkled white button-down the front shirts, several pairs of thin black socks and my mother's old house dresses. The drawer contained things least often used but not ready to be thrown away yet. Satisfied that I knew the contents of the drawer that I had rambled through many times before, I closed it. I retrieved a straight-backed chair from the back porch to explore the next drawer.

The distinctive smell of my mother's nylon slips and night gowns filled my nose. The smell made me wonder. *Is this odor my mother's natural scent or the material? Or is this what my mother and this material smell like together?* I felt the thickness of several white bras and examined my mother's white nylon underpants and wondered why the crotches were yellowed. My mother's drawer full of clothing made me ask myself questions about my own life to come. *When will I wear a bra? Does stuff come out of women down there that stains their underpants?* I did not yet wear nylon underclothing or a nylon sleep gown. I wore cotton things. I closed the drawer and finally looked through the third drawer.

While Lee and Dale remained absorbed in the lives of the characters in the movie on television, I on this Saturday morning without my parents, felt a compulsion to ramble through drawers in search of unknown clues about my family.

In the last dresser drawer, along with Daddy's white t-shirts, striped boxer shorts and worn tube socks, I found a half-empty, store-bought bottle of gin and a box of hore-hound candy of which I had two pieces. After satisfying my urge to search, by assuring myself I knew the contents of the drawers, I rejoined Lee and Dale by the television.

∞

When my parents returned from their jaunt, they seemed changed. Both were in good moods. My mother seemed foggy, less sharp, softened just a little. A "Sugar" came out of her mouth in reference to the youngest of us. A slow smile crossed my father's face when he talked to us. They seemed cozy while the same smells as from the liquor bottles outside earlier in the day swirled about them.

For the rest of Saturday, Mama tended a large pot of pinto beans with ham hocks between naps. Daddy left home sev-eral times in the truck. Each time he returned, he harassed my mother more intensely until he exploded, "Get your lazy ass out of bed and fix some dinner."

By early evening, the words that made me sick to my stomach thundered out of his mouth. "All you do is eat, shit and sleep." My brothers and I watched him shout at our mother in her reclined position on the bed until she dragged herself to her feet.

After a full day of intermittent play and watching my par-ents transform into their weekend selves, my brothers and I drifted off to sleep as we huddled in our bed together. Sud-denly we were startled to wakefulness with the sound of loud voices. His voice was deep and thunderous, hers slow and growling. Back and forth they volleyed words. I tried not to hear. I squeezed my eyes shut and covered my ears.

Even with my hands on my ears, I heard them. My brothers and I lay still, stiff with quietness, no breathing noises or scratching or coughing.

The sound of something crashing and breaking stimulated the three of us to our feet. We scrambled through the bedroom doorway into the room where our parents flung pieces of our mismatched china at one another. My favorite plates with the blue drawings on them, the tan ones, and some translucent green coffee cups sailed through the air.

Lee and I shouted, "Stop. Stop Mama. Daddy." Dale and I cried.

As usual Lee commanded, "Stop crying!"

I dried my tears but Dale stood wet-faced, rubbing his eyes and mumbling about their fighting. Another dish exploded on the wall. Dale cried louder. I shielded my head with my arms. I did not know then that this fight would be the last fight where my mother would stand her ground against our father.

Our parents noticed us. Daddy's forty-nine-year-old self with three young children and a twenty-nine-year old wife stopped to stare at us. Mama turned and said in our direction, "It's okay."

They huffed with nervous rasping in their breathing. Their eyes darted around the room taking in the sight of their two crying children, the broken dishes, but not each other's eyes. Mama went to Dale. "Come here." She lifted him onto her hip. She walked away, unsteadily, out of the room through the kitchen to the back porch. Lee followed asking, "What're you and Daddy fighting about Mama?"

My father sat down on the bench that served as his children's seats at the dinner table. He put his hands to his forehead and rubbed at the sweat and the tiredness on his face. He twisted his mouth and gnashed his teeth together. A slight stream of blood trickled down his upper arm, slowly, over his dark brown skin. He smudged the blood with his hand and did not notice. I went to him barefooted, dodging chunks of glass and put my five-year-old arm on his shoulder and said, "Daddy your arm is bleeding." My nose was stuffy and puffy and my cheeks burned from heat and salty tears.

"I know, I know," he said as if it didn't matter. I put my head on my father's shoulder to console him. Mama returned with a broom. "Get out of here. You'll cut your feet." She fanned the broom in the direction of the bedroom door.

I tiptoed out of the dining room and into the kitchen. I felt a sting from my toe. I hopped to a seated position on the floor and rubbed my hand over the bottom of my foot. I pulled a tiny white sliver of glass from my big toe and flung it into the air. A mound of blood appeared. I squeezed the bleeding spot. "I've got glass in my foot," I yelled but nobody came to check me. I sat there on the worn vinyl-covered floor, alone, in my own buzz of spongy distance from everyone and everything around me.

6

The yellow school bus pulled off the Star section of Highway 220 onto the hard, rocky, red-soiled patch of ground
where Mama, Lee and I stood. The doors flapped open. Lee
boarded first and greeted the driver who was a sinewy black
man. "Morning Mr. James." The driver responded with a
head nod at Lee and returned a morning greeting. The
warmth of the bus caressed my chilled face and hands as I
climbed the steps to board and smiled at Mr. James. He nodded at me.

When Mama boarded she said, "How you doing Mr.
James?" She sat with me and Lee on a seat near the front of
the bus. I looked around. The bus was less than a quarter
filled with quiet, brown-complexioned children. I suspected
that I was the only child going to my first day of first grade,
as there were no other parents on the bus.

Mr. James pulled a handle that made the doors swoosh
then click closed. We passed Joe Britt's vegetable market
that Mama, my brothers and I had walked to several times
the previous summer. J.F. Allen's construction company,
where my father worked, was on the border of Biscoe and
Star. We passed the white kid's school.

In Biscoe, the bus gathered children from the two black neighborhoods. With the exception of four or five of them whose families we visited sometimes and the Goldstone kids, everyone else was unfamiliar to me.

I watched each child step onto the bus. I noticed that each girl and boy was some shade of brown, either toward a lighter mocha or as dark as coffee beans. I wore my hair in two ponytails and most of the girls my age wore their hair plaited in braids. Each boy's hair was cut short on the sides with a thicker patch left on top and a part cut into one side or the other. Mama, Lee and I stood out being the lightest people on the bus. I fidgeted. Mama told me, "Sit still."

Many of the Biscoe children said *hey* to Lee as though they were old buddies. In a matter of minutes and miles, he went from belonging to me and my mother to belonging to them. I did not like the feeling of losing his attention. I felt alone and wished he would talk with me. When the children's chatter became loud, Mr. James looked back through his rear-view mirror and said in a bold and firm voice, "Quiet down now."

With the exception of going into the two black sections of Biscoe and down State Road 24/27 by the drive-in to pick up the Goldstones, we traveled Highway 220 from Star through Biscoe and into Candor. Our destination was Brutonville, Montgomery County's black elementary school.

∞

Once off the bus, a chubby girl guided by her older sibling headed in the same direction as Mama and I. The older girl acted adult-like though she was Lee's age. "You must be

Lee's Mama," she said as she looked up at my mother. "I'm in his grade. I'm Emmalene and this is Ola Mae. She's in the first grade. Mrs. Martin's room." Ola Mae smiled shyly.

"Mrs. Martin is Levonne's teacher too. You're going to be classmates." Mama spoke sweetly as she looked from me to Ola Mae. I had never seen a fat child before and could not take my eyes from Ola Mae's round medium brown cheeks, her short braids and her body that reminded me of the Pillsbury Dough Boy on television commercials. Mama and Emmalene talked as Ola Mae and I walked along quietly.

When the multi-hued kids in Mrs. Martin's classroom saw me, they approached quickly with curious looks on their faces. One dark-skinned boy said, "She's white!" His comment caused a flurry of chatter. I tightened my grip on Mama's hand and she mine. Mrs. Martin fanned the children back to their seats and acted as though nothing had been said. This was the first time that I had been referred to as *white* by anyone, and I judged by the astounded expression of the child who made the observation out loud, being *white* was a freaky thing. After Mama watched Emmalene turn Ola Mae over to the teacher, she greeted Mrs. Martin, a honey-brown, stout woman with a warm personality.

"Good morning, Mrs. Martin. How you doing?"

"I'm just fine. Who do we have here?"

"This is Robert Lee's sister. Levonne." Mama nudged me toward the teacher dressed in a matching grey knit jacket and skirt with black pumps. I shied back toward Mama.

"Good morning, Levonne. Welcome to the first grade."

Mrs. Martin gave me a smile and directed that I could go over to a low table where other children sat. Mama encouraged me with a little nudge. I took a few hesitant steps, and then looked back to see my mother turning to leave. I ran to her and took her hand.

"Oh no, you're going to stay," Mama smiled at the teacher while throwing her a *we-know-what's-going-on-here* look.

Mrs. Martin said, "Levonne, come play with the other children. We're going to have a good time today."

I looked into my mama's face and she had a look of concern about her that I believed I should not abandon. The look said to me, *this is as hard for me as it is for you.* So I persisted in following her.

The two adults' eyes met again. Mrs. Martin whispered something to my mother then directed me with her hand on my shoulder to a table with bright colors of paints in plastic jars. Children sat at the table and dabbed ice cream sticks, with the wet paint on the ends, onto white paper. By the time I turned back to look at Mama from being mesmerized by the girls, their bulky braided hair and their colored papers, she was gone.

Alone, on my own, in the strange place I had dreamed about going to, I saw that it was different than I had imagined. I had pictured kids that looked like Lee. I imagined children with light skin and black curly hair like his. I had not imagined the sea of brown faces or all the dark brown eyes that studied me. I was immobilized by the sight of paint-splattered hands that reached out to touch my pony tails.

When Mrs. Martin greeted another parent, the children came at me the way they might have gone at a basket of new puppies. "Her hair feels like my doll's hair" and "her eyes are the color of my doll's." The kids surrounded me and petted my hair and skin until I sweated and squirmed as new puppies might in the strange hands and beneath the hot breaths of children not familiar with how to treat such a thing yet.

"Children. Leave Levonne alone." Mrs. Martin scattered the children with her voice back to their places. I felt swoony. "Let's sit down children." Mrs. Martin clapped her hands. The attention of the morning embarrassed me and made me feel different in a way that I had not felt before. Rather than focus on the children, I turned my attention to Mrs. Martin's every movement.

But one boy in my class would not allow me to ignore him. A dark-complexioned boy with almond-shaped eyes spoke with a nasally northern tone. "Cat eyes. Cat eyes. You've got cat eyes," he accused.

"I do not."

"You do. Your eyes look just like my cat's eyes!"

The truth may have been that my hazel gray, green eyes were closer in color to a cat's than to the dark brown eyes of all my classmates, but I could not bear to think that then. Tears swelled in my eyes from the insult.

One girl said, "Mrs. Martin, that boy said she has cat eyes."

Mrs. Martin looked at me and at the boy. "Young man! You stop that talk right now! People have their eyes and cats have theirs. I don't want to hear you saying that again."

Mrs. Martin's words meant that I was as human as the boy and this meant to me that I was as good as anyone, regardless of my freaky eyes. I turned my attention back to her and gladly went to a desk at the front of the classroom, as she directed when it was time for us to get started with learning.

∞

I went about first grade loving to learn the alphabet, to read books from the modest school library, and to count, but with an ongoing awareness that I was different than the other kids. I had the lightest complexion and eyes, the straightest hair, and was the youngest in the class. My looks made me stand out and made me feel uncomfortable, odd.

One day about a month after school had begun, Mrs. Martin clicked the hard yellow chalk against the blackboard and said out loud the letters that made the name of the story she was about to read to us. "The Ugly Duckling," she pronounced slowly. "Come on children. Say it with me." She clicked the chalk against the board next to each syllable of each word until every mouth was moving and every voice was audible.

The desks were lined in rows of six. The desk surfaces were smooth, light tan colored and contrasted with the thin brown arms and hands that reached across them and fidgeted while awaiting the start of the story. Some children bounced in their seats enough to make the small desks slip out of alignment. Voices mumbled in high and low pitches. Mrs. Martin's voice was calm. She focused on the book she was holding.

"Quiet now, children." A wave of increasing silence

washed over the group as she displayed the book above her head. Everyone waited for what the teacher had in store for them.

The story commenced. What unfolded was something incredible. Amidst ducklings in shades of grey, brown and black was a little gangly white bird that was supposed to be their sibling. I looked around the room. My vision filled with the images of the multiple shades of brown that were my classmates' faces, arms and legs. I looked at my own arms against the tan desk top and did not see the same distinct difference between arm color and desktop.

I returned my attention to Mrs. Martin. The story of oddness unfolded and at first I felt so ashamed that I wanted to put my head in a paper bag and hide there forever. I was sure that my classmates were watching me and laughing to themselves at me. Then something happened that made all the difference. The ugly white duckling discovered that it was a swan and grew up to be more beautiful than any of the ducks. The faded little bird had not ever been ugly, just mistaken for something that it was not. The story changed me. I realized that I was a swan. I was certain that I was in for a bright future.

7

"Stop that!" Daddy warned me and my brothers again from his spot on the long sofa that placed him across from the black and white Zenith. Dinner had already been eaten and darkness owned the sky space outside. We children quieted the noise from our play.

My parents' eyes were intent on the television screen. Pictures of a firebombed bus with black people standing and sitting beside it, talk of blacks in Atlanta sitting at restaurant counters and whites being mad at them, and John F. Kennedy talked about being the president of the United States.

It was the winter of my first year of school. Lee and Dale continued to toss the head of my bride doll back and forth. The head belonged to my favorite doll. She had short hair with curl enough to make her look sophisticated even as all the play made it a little tousled-looking too. It had become a common game between my brothers to toss the doll's head like a ball around the room. Sometimes I hated the game and felt assaulted by the destruction of my doll, and other times it seemed the right thing to be doing. That evening, it felt right enough. We squealed again in childish excitement as the doll's head flew through the cigarette-smoky living room warmed by the wood stove.

When the report on the television moved from the fire-bombed bus to the Winter Olympics at Squaw Valley in California, with pictures of skiers gliding down a snow covered mountain, Daddy warned again, "Stop that." He stood from the sofa and my mother watched as my brothers flung my doll's head yet again. Lee missed Dale's pitch. Our father scooped the doll head from the corner where it landed and in a quick motion with his hankerchief to protect his hand from the hot metal, raised the lid of the woodstove and popped the doll's head into the hot burning fire.

Lee and Dale began another form of horseplay, but I lay on the cool, vinyl-covered floor on my stomach and, as I often did, positioned myself to peer inside the stove through the spaces between the open draft cups and the metal of the stove frame. I watched the heat melt my doll's hair first, then her pink face. Nobody said a word about the smell of cooking plastic that tinged the air of the room. Within a day, I had developed head sores. Nobody could figure out the origin of the lesions. I threw my doll's body in a pile of trash in the weeds behind our house. I was too old for a doll anyway.

∞

Cold crept in around the curtainless window frames and through the glass. Wind created crumpling-metal sounds from the tin roof. Nip was in the air outside, on the grayed tree branches, the brown leaves, and on the grey-black earth's surface. Daddy chopped fire wood from short logs of pine, oak and cedar. Lee at eight years old and I at six carried armloads of wood inside and placed it beside the living room and kitchen stoves.

The sides of the living room stove turned red in spots from the hot burning wood. The red looked redder than anything I had ever seen. The edges of the red spread bigger over the side of the metal stove. After reaching a brilliant fire red that pulsed and mesmerized me, the hot spot shrank and ended as a white powdery finish over the black metal sides. I loved watching the stove get red and yet I was afraid too. What if I slipped and burned my hand on the hot stove, or if the heat melted the side of the stove, allowing the inside fire to tumble out into the room? I feared that the hot spot would grow and grow and become bigger than me, which in my mind made it stronger than me.

And then the most awful thing happened. While Lee and I moved checkers around on the game's scuffed board, Mama rested in a straight-backed chair beside the fired stove in our living room. She held four-year-old Dale. He was loose and floppy from the sleep that had overtaken him in Mama's arms. Mama's body was loose from a sleepiness that came from being toasty-warmed by the fire and from the white lightning liquor that she had been sipping behind everyone's back. She nodded, then caught herself the way sitting-up sleepers do at some critical point when their body is startled out of where it is going, when their body has gotten too far out of balance and gravity grabs it at the same time as the body grabs itself back.

And then it happened. The warmth, the alcohol effect,

the sleep, and the gravity came into perfect unison. Mama toppled forward toward the stove and let my brother's sleeping face fall against the side of it. Mama startled and Dale screamed from the hot that burned his brown cheek.

I watched with eyes wide open in terror as Mama took our family's baby back under her power and control. She woke from the deepest sleep, fought through fogginess as thick as cold ocean water over a drowning person's head, and pulled him back against her chest. Dale was in trouble. We were all in trouble.

The experience of Mama, Dale and the stove taught me that our family, and that I as much as our youngest child, were in serious danger when our mother drank. A line of carelessness had been crossed with devastating consequence.

8

In my sixth year, when winter turned into spring, tender yellow green emerged from every tree, grass and weed which, in my mind, made the world a magic place. I had taken to going into the woods on my own, preferring nature and the world of my mind to the company of my family.

The harshness of the past winter left scars. One was on my four-year-old brother Dale's face. His right cheek showed the marks from being burned by the hot wood stove. Another was in my heart from hearing my brother's cry from the pain of the burn and watching his brown skin harden to a scab and ooze puss and blood before finally healing.

The place in the woods that I found to escape my family felt vast and cozy. A grove of middle-aged pine trees left an opening at their collective tops where sunshine shone in onto a mossy carpet and through which blue sky with white clouds could be seen. It was a special place with pine tree needle and bark smells. Robins, cardinals, blue birds chirped all around.

In the grove, if there was a strong enough breeze blowing, the trees swirled and their trunks moved like beverage stirrer sticks pushed about in a glass of liquid. The stirring created a soft swooshing movement all around, that for a six-year old may have been reminiscent of the sensation once felt when cradled and rocked to sleep by a mother.

The magic in the pine tree grove came from the moss that had grown on the forest floor where the sun shone. Clumps of small, soft plant stems grew close together to create a natural and strong bed, larger than the one I slept in at night.

There on the moss carpet, I snuggled in, tucking my legs and body into a tight ball. I listened to the forest sounds–wind, birds chirping, a deer cracking a stick with its hoof—until what I was hearing took over and become everything. I was safe. Peaceful inside and out. The tight ball who was me loosened as I relaxed there with the earth and forest smells. My body rested upon the bed of moss, supported by the solid ground beneath.

After a while in my wilderness, I felt the lift of a magic carpet, heard the whispers of fairies and elves, sensed the presence of friendly animals, and imagined Sleeping Beauty's bed, with me, as her, resting upon it. There I lay, waiting to be awakened by a protective prince that would carry me far away to a beautiful and perfect world.

∞

The summer Wednesday morning started out iridescent blue gold, the way a flame from a gas range is blue gold—the blue center of the flame, having the appearance of coolness. The edges gold, warmer. The flame bids you touch it. It looks harmless before you put your hands into it.

It was the summer of my sixth year. I had completed first

grade at Brutonville Elementary School. My father was at his dollar-ten-cents-an-hour construction company laborer's job.

Lee, Dale and I spread the plastic from Daddy's job out in the grass, dumped buckets of water on it drawn from our well, then launched ourselves onto the slick surface and skidded like tires tossed on ice. Mama smoked Salems and contemplatively watched us from the porch. Caressing warmth shone from her eyes as it did from the sun. The white smoke from her cigarette circled around her, then dissolved into the air.

Mama's view of us changed many times through a day and that Wednesday was no different. Her mood was a soft pale yellow early in the day–quiet, slow, eggs and fatback for breakfast, served with cold leftover biscuits. The paleness shifted to a spiked yellow orange at times throughout the day when we took our rowdiness too close to her. "Y'all go somewhere else with that racket!"

Outside in the blue gold world of sky, air, and sunlight, moist with water and sweat, my brothers and I knocked against one another, then slipped and slid our bodies along the plastic. The three of us were a hot bundle of energy set to explode many times yet in the day.

Our attention shifted from one another and the water play to a white finned Pontiac that appeared on the rocky road ambling its way toward our house. Clayton came often to visit. On this particular summer day, he came to mow the tough grass that my father's hand-powered mower could not handle.

Clayton was taller than either my mother or my father by many inches. He was a slim man, sinewy. He wore the blue striped-denim cap of railroad workers and had given Daddy one of those caps. This tall, dark, brown-eyed friend of my parents traveled away from his family sometimes for weeks to work on the railroad tracks that took clacking trains through small North Carolina towns. I could not imagine a daddy not coming home from work everyday.

Clayton flashed us a smile from the driver's seat of his car and as he opened the door said, "You children enjoying being out of school?" We clambered around him as he unloaded the mower from the trunk of his car. Smells of gasoline, cut grass, and engine oil mingled in my nose as he poured liquid fuel into the mower from a smudged, white plastic jug. Mama joined us by the car.

The two exchanged greetings as usual, my mother smiling and smoothing the black braids she had wrapped around her head and smelling of the McNess Man's body powder. Clayton responded with a slow pace and deep tone. To a child anticipating the excitement of tall grass being mowed, the interaction between them seemed little more than warm background noise.

We all watched as Clayton jerked the mower backward to dislodge large clumps of chewed green that repeatedly choked the roar into silence. Over and over he yanked the cord to start the mower, then returned to obliterate the mass of growth, small sections at a time. Though my brothers and I were content to watch the struggle between man, machine and plant, our mother insisted that we pick blackberries from the woods surrounding our house.

"Awe, Ma! Can't we do that later?" We protested.

"You want blackberry dumplings, don't you?" It was more a command than a question.

Unwillingly, Lee and I took two plastic pails by their wire handles and departed the yard. Dale followed behind, empty-handed and struggling to keep up. We knew where to find every creek, each grove of long-needle pine, and the thick beds of cool moss. We knew where to find giant saw-dust piles left over from sawmills long since closed, aban-doned tobacco barns, persimmon trees and blackberry patches.

A trip into the woods was an adventure, an exploration bound by nothing but our physical abilities and mutual will-ingness. But on that Wednesday, we headed straight for the nearest berry patch.

From the bushes on the edge of a sunny clearing, we half filled the two buckets and ate fewer berries than usual, and then rushed back toward home. On that day, Lee and I were more irritated than usual with tag-along Dale's smaller steps and less agile movements. "Hurry up Peebag," we repri-manded.

∞

Initially we noticed the absence of lawn mower noise. Once in clear view of our house, we noticed the absence of Mama and Clayton. Onto the porch we bounded with our buckets swinging violently. I was the first to reach the front screened door. Grabbing the handle and pulling, my hand hurt as it slipped off and scraped the metal.

"Move." Lee was irritated with me for failing to open the door. He tugged the handle and experienced the same resistance. He put his hand against the screen to shade an area to peer through. "Mama!" Lee's tone was assertive for an eight-year-old.

Mama's voice tumbled out to us. "You didn't get those berries picked yet!" Dale and I joined Lee in making a shaded area with our hands to peer through the screened door that I had no memory of ever having been locked. Though we could not see Mama, we heard her voice from a room in the rear of our house. I checked Lee's face for clues to what was going on. The locked door with Mama and Clayton inside meant something was wrong, though I did not know for sure what. Lee knocked on the door frame more forcefully. "Go get more blackberries!" Mama commanded. This was not her usual command to get out from under her feet. This was different. We were not disturbing her quiet or her sanity; it was something with Clayton that we were disturbing.

"Ma I'm thirsty. I want to come in." I knocked on the door frame rapidly, feeling a sense of urgency. But there was no response.

Lee turned, swung the plastic pail around in a way that forced berries to spill onto the porch. A loud bashing hop on both legs down each of three wooden steps forced more berries out of his pail. Dale and I followed, me stepping on each berry that Lee had spilled, squishing it into the wood,

76

turning the soles of my feet into a purple stamp that made Rorschach designs as I walked.

∞

Later in the day, when allowed inside our house, Clayton exited as I entered. I looked at my mother and she at me, both of us wordless. Inside, I noticed our couch draped with the same usually-crumpled-from-kids'-play faded bedspread. The cover was tucked into the crevasses of the couch and was as smooth as the surface of calm water. In the center of the spread was a fresh wet spot the size of an egg. The neatness of the spread and the wet spot registered in my mind as a puzzle to be solved. I looked again at my mother who asked Lee, "Where are the berries? " Not understanding why, I surmised my mother weakened the threads that bound my family together that day. I decided that I would have nothing to do with her blackberry dumplings ever again.

∞

When Daddy arrived home, we ran to him as usual and I unlaced and pulled off his work boots for him. "Hi Daddy. Can I see what you have in your pockets?" As he had for years before, he let me ramble through the bib overall pockets. I found the tablet where he kept his hours worked for J.F. Allen recorded, a stubby pencil sharpened by a dull butcher knife, two sticks of Juicy Fruit gum, and a small round green can labeled Doan's Kidney Pills. I sat in my daddy's lap, chewed Juicy Fruit and listened as he asked my mother about the day.

"Clayton mowed the yard today?"

"Um hum. No more wet feet and clothes from the dew on the grass. Finally."

"We picked blackberries, Daddy." I interjected.

"Yeah. Blackberry dumplings for dessert," my mother said. "Why don't you leave your daddy alone, Levonne, and go out and play."

I remained sitting in my father's lap, determined that I would not mind my mother. I had my father's protection. I hugged him around his neck and took in the smell of sweat and sawdust in my father's t-shirt.

"Mama locked us out of the house today, Daddy," I whined with my face buried in his shirt. My mother was quiet. My father did not respond. I looked at the two of them to find them both looking not at one another but off into the distance with blank eyes.

∞

My father, driven by his wild Saturday energy, cooked all day while Mama became groggier and took naps. By the time we were ready to sit down to eat the green beans cooked in water and fatback, the fried chicken, and the peach pie made in the top lid of the turkey roasting pan with Wonder bread slices as a crust, our father yelled those words I hated in Mama's direction.

"Get up! You're no good for nothing but to eat, shit and sleep." As usual my stomach knotted and I felt tremendous shame. I looked at the green beans shining from the fat and felt my world all out of whack. And at the same time, it felt normal because this was how it was on weekends at my house.

I tasted things slowly so as not to gag. Before he sat, Daddy stomped into the bedroom and pulled Mama from the bed. She walked unsteadily into the dining room and looked perturbed and uncoordinated. My brothers and I sat trying to eat the food our father had made for us, along with trying to ignore what was going on between them.

In an angry flash, Daddy pinned Mama against the refrigerator. His hands pressed hard against her throat. She tried to pull his hands away. When her hands dropped to her side and her eyes rolled upward, Lee and I leapt up. We both yelled words at our parents. *She's dying and he's killing her* I thought. I had witnessed strangulation deaths on television.

"Stop Daddy," Lee insisted as Dale cried.

"Don't hurt her," I pleaded.

"I'm not." My father's teeth were clinched together. He was puffing hard.

My brothers and I yelled our separate pleas together like a chorus. Lee looked mad. He wanted my father to stop but he, being young and trained to respect his parents, by the parents that he was watching, could not take action except to look mad. Mama's eyes rolled around and her eyelids fluttered. She gagged. On tip toes, I hopped up and down in place. "No Daddy. No." I felt alone as though my brothers were not there. As though my parents were going, melting into nothing before my eyes. *Mama is about to die* I told myself. I had never felt that degree of insanity in my world.

Then Daddy turned Mama loose. She slid down the side of the refrigerator onto the floor. He looked down at her. Mama slumped over her raised knees. I ran the few steps to my mother. "Mama. Get up." I wanted her to move normally. She raised her head and raised herself from a seated position on the floor to a standing position.

On that evening I realized that even though I had trouble with my mother's ways, I did not want her dead. I wanted my mother on that evening, with all her problems, more than anything in the world. I also knew that I could not be, nor should I ever want to be, the passive recipient Mama had become of my father's actions.

9

I already had two brothers. One was five and the other, nine years old. I was seven when the new baby was born. By winter 1961, I was ready for a new sibling, though I was most ready for a sister. I dreamed of combing her hair, of playing tea time and dolls together, of having girl secrets from the boys. We needed another female in our family to make it equal girls to boys. Even when I was little I knew things were best when there was balance.

I was disappointed when I heard that the new baby was a boy. He was premature, "born too early," our father told us while Mama was still in the hospital. *More of the same* I thought. *Boys, BB guns, wrestling around the house. No Mama's jewelry or movie-star-dresses playmate. I am on my own.* I felt sad and lonely for the sister I had made in my dreams. I was angry too.

Daddy said playfully, "He's a small fry. We might wan' to throw him back."

"Yeah!" I agreed without explaining that I would trade the premature boy in a minute for a girl.

When Mama returned home from the hospital, I asked, "Why didn't we get a girl? I don't want another boy."

"God decides about that," she said. "God knows best."

"What? Does God think it's best for me to be alone as a sister?" I was indignant. My mother explained that I was lucky to have brothers that would always look out for me, that would always help me if I was in trouble, that would fight for me against anybody. I did not think that this was a good trade for a sister, I told her. She said that I was hopeless and ungrateful and selfish and that this was not a good way to be. Mama said that God knows best and that was that. Over and done. When Mama was done with a thing, she was done and she expected you to be done with it too. You knew she was not going to talk with you about your silliness any more, and she was not going to like you if you talked about it.

Trying to resign myself to having another brother, I asked Mama when the premature baby was coming home. "He has to gain two more pounds and then we can have him."

Though I continued to struggle over not having a sister, I did not tire of hearing about a baby in an incubator. I was interested in how long it took babies to gain a pound, what did premature mean, what made a baby born premature?

"Born before his body is ready to be born," is how Mama described premature. "Before he grows big enough and his heart and lungs are developed well enough." An incubator helped the baby stay warm and cozy while his body and organs kept growing.

Mama said that she was not sure that this baby was premature. She said she thought he might just be small. She said that in her mind the time she carried him added up to

82

nine months. I was young then and thought nothing of the incongruence between the hospital's explanation of my little brother's problems and Mama's calculation. I would not learn of reasons for a full-term baby appearing to be premature until I was an adult. The medical profession did not have a concept or the word for Fetal Alcohol Syndrome in 1961.

I pictured the little baby brother under a warm light, squirming about and growing. After all, it was winter and a cold North Carolina January at that. The sky had one big grey cloud covering the blue. The trees were bare and looked like bundles of sticks clumped together.

My mind was not on second grade at Brutonville Elementary after Christmas break. Upon learning that the baby was almost ready to come home, I asked my mother "Can we get him if the roads ice?" I imagined the baby weighing all that he needed to weigh, ready to leave the hospital and because of the ice on the roads, my parents not able to drive to get him. I knew that babies needed mamas and I knew that we needed the baby. Things were already feeling out of whack from the family waiting for him. Daddy and Mama snapped at each other even on weekdays. Daddy carried a mad look on his face most all the time. Mama looked uneasy. Lee was on top of five-year-old Dale wrestling until Dale cried several times each day. I watched everyone and knew that my family was going to break if something didn't happen soon. Mama didn't seem to have enough oomph to accomplish cooking a dinner at night.

I decided to help make things easier for my parents by

emptying the pee jars first thing in the morning and getting the wood in first thing after school without being told. Since Mama did not seem able to get things done in a day, I also swept the floor and washed the dishes for her. Although I was sure that Daddy and Mama would smile and say *Oh how great! The chores are done and the house cleaned. All because our little Levonne swept the floor, washed the dishes, brought in the wood and emptied the slop jars!* But neither of them said a word. While feeling hurt and angry over the whole predicament, I kept helping, just so that my family would seem some kind of normal to me.

∞

On the second Wednesday after Christmas break, Lee and I returned from school to find my mother holding the new baby wrapped in a blue blanket. The room was warm from the stove's fire. The little creature's fingers and arms moved about in aimless motions. His eyes were open, little slits with black inside. He had hair enough to let you know a little about the curls to come. He was small. Smaller than my baby dolls. His skin was pinkish-white. He was beautiful to me.

On his first day with us, between the time of my arriving home from school and our family going to bed, the baby slept. The next morning, when I awoke between Lee and Dale, I discovered the baby was in my parents' bed. An animal-like little cry came from under the covers that were propped up like a tent. It was cold enough to see my breath in the bedroom where our family slept. *Can the baby breathe under there?* I wondered. *Is there enough air for him? Will Mama*

84

smother him to death if she keeps him under the covers too long?
This was a curious and worrisome business.

Usually on a weekday, Daddy was already gone to work
by the time Mama woke me and Lee to get ready for school.
Instead, there we were, all at home and not going anywhere
because it was too icy outside. My brothers squirmed and
wiggled around in the bed on both sides of me. I wanted
them to get still so that the covers would stop lifting and
puffing cold air onto me. I told Mama that she needed to
tell Lee and Dale to stop messing around. She did not say
a word. So I repeated louder, "Mama make Lee and Dale
stop!"

Mama poked her head from under the covers. "Stop it
now! All of you! Get up and get your clothes on." I was
glad to get up. I jumped out from between the toasty place
between my brothers and tiptoed fast over the cold wood
floor to Mama's bed and asked if I could see the baby. She
told me in a snappy way, "Get your clothes on." So I grabbed
some things to wear as quickly as lightning strikes and followed the smell of breakfast food into the kitchen.

Daddy stood in front of the wood stove in his work
clothes. Blue overalls, plaid shirt, work boots. He put ham
into a cast iron frying pan. The meat sizzled and made a salty
smelling puff of steam with each new piece that he laid in
the pan. He was not paying any attention to me.

"You not going to work, Daddy?"

"No. Too much ice."

I warmed my clothes one piece at a time by the heat of
the stove before putting them on. Then I read the floor's

linoleum rug designs of printed nursery rhymes and illustrations, worn from all the feet that had tracked over them. Daddy listened. He had stopped going to school before he learned to read for himself.

"Humpty Dumpty sat on a wall." I looked at Daddy and he looked back at me. He smiled and turned the pieces of sizzling meat. My nose filled with the nutty smell of the meat cooking as I read on. "Little Miss Muffat sat on her tuffet." I skipped to another picture. "Old King Cole was a merry old soul."

Mama brought the new brother wrapped in a warm blanket into the kitchen. Lee and Dale tumbled out of the bedroom behind her, nearly knocking her feet from under her.

"Cut that racket out right now," Daddy wolfed at them. "Close that door. You're letting all the heat out." Lee closed the door between the bedroom and the kitchen. Mama sat by the stove in a straight-backed chair. I made my place standing beside her while Lee and Dale struggled to pull pants on over the underwear they had slept in, and long-sleeve shirts on over the t-shirts that doubled as pajama tops.

I watched the small face of the baby that shone from underneath the cover. *Maybe he is small* I thought. I wondered what the proper size of babies was supposed to be. He had a cute little nose.

Mama unwrapped the blanket from around the baby's legs to check his diaper. I ran my finger over his skin. He was soft, so much softer than the hard plastic of dolls. *He's beautiful* I thought. *More beautiful than any thing I have ever seen.*

My mother gave no resistance to my maneuvering the baby from her.

"Hold his head there in the crook of your arm." She arranged the baby in my arms then rose from her chair to give her space to me. I wanted this baby for my own.

∞

"We have to name him." Mama reached for the aluminum pan that we all used to wash our faces in the morning.

I held the baby and watched my father crack eggs into a bowl. "Daddy what do you want to call him?" I asked.

Everyone was quiet as we waited to hear the name he had in mind for his newest son. My father looked at us but not at any one in particular. "Call him what you want." With those words, he pushed the frying pan to the edge of the stove where it was less hot, then lifted the wood box from beside the stove and went outside. The sound of his harking and spitting to clear his sinuses trailed back at us from the woodpile.

During my father's absence from the kitchen that he had made warm with fire and delicious with ham smells, my brothers and I began the task of naming our newest sibling. Mama checked the ham in the black cast-iron frying pan. She placed leftover biscuits in the oven to warm. Over the sound of Daddy chopping wood on the other side of the kitchen window, the conversation progressed.

"Let's name him after Uncle Frank," I said.

"Frank?" Lee asked.

I looked at the baby in my arms. I felt his warmth. "Franklin."

"He needs two names," Lee insisted. "Everybody else has two names." Mama stirred the eggs that my father had cracked into the bowl. "What about after Uncle James too?"

"Franklin James?" I said.

"No, James Frank," five-year old Dale added.

Mama said, "How about James Franklin?" We all thought and agreed that James Franklin was a good name.

"We can call him Frankie." I excitedly added, "And his initials will be the same as J.F. Allen."

"Hey yeah," Lee agreed. "And J.F. Kennedy too."

Uncle James was Daddy's brother that was dead and who I did not know. We had a picture of Uncle James on our wall in the dining room that I stretched my neck to see. Alone in the black and white photograph, Uncle James stood skinny and tall with long arms. His hair was wavy black. His skin was dark, smooth and leathery. I imagined him in one of those feather headdresses that Indian Chiefs wore. I looked back at the baby and asked, "Frankie? Do you like that name?"

Uncle Frank was married to Daddy's sister, Aunt Janie. That uncle and aunt were my favorite relatives. Uncle Frank and Aunt Janie always gave us money when they visited. Pennies, nickels, dimes. My parents said that Uncle Frank traded his old car for a new Cadillac every year. I imagined Frankie and me riding in Uncle Frank's clean and shiny car.

J.F. This letter combination was doubly good for Frankie's name. J.F. Allen was my daddy's *white* brother and was the man he worked for. Daddy started working for J.F.'s parents when he was eleven years old. Mamu and Papa were getting another colored grandchild, but one with the same initials as their real son.

Finally, when it came to my brother's name, the J.F. stood for John Fitzgerald as in our brand new President Kennedy's name. He was a man that was going to be good for colored people, my parents said. I was proud that J.F. Kennedy, J.F. Allen, Uncle James and Uncle Frank all had a part in my brother's name.

Upon my father's return to the kitchen with a full box of wood, Dale said, "We're calling him Frankie for short, Daddy."

Our father's response was, "Good. Get your shoes on. You're gonna end up with colds."

I puzzled over why Daddy was disinterested in naming this new child in our family. I decided that he had already named two boys and a girl and guessed that it was no fun for him anymore. I may not have understood about my father's attitude, but I knew for sure that Frankie was special and that he would need every bit of attention from me that I was set to shower on a sister.

∞

Without a sister at home, I was ripe for a best girlfriend. Teresa Johnson skipped second grade, which made her the youngest in our third grade class. Teresa was eleven months and two weeks younger than me. Prior to Teresa, I had been the youngest in our class. And I had not had a best friend during my first two years at Brutonville Elementary. On the first day in Mrs. Justice's third grade, Teresa approached me and examined my curls and my clothes with her eyes and hands. From that moment, she claimed me as hers and that was how it began.

∞

Though younger, Teresa had a presence about her that was beyond her years. She was confident, forceful, and always knew what she wanted. This may have developed from the privileged position of being a teacher's daughter. Her mother was one of the fourth grade teachers at Brutonville.

Mrs. Johnson was tall and beautiful. She wore a deep hue of lip color that set off the brown in her skin and her pressed, curled hair. Mrs. Johnson's sleepy eyes made her look sexy. She was young and shapely and all of us wished we had a mother as smart and pretty as Teresa's.

Whereas Mrs. Johnson had a sophisticated quality about her, Teresa was more of a bull. With pug nose and round face, no matter how Teresa's hair was fixed, she and it always looked the same. Frazzled. Her straightened hair stuck this way and that. She seemed to always overfill her clothes.

∞

Though I did not know it on the first day of meeting Teresa, she and her family were going to be life savers for me at a time when my own family was as unstable as the ocean's surface during a storm. While my parents seemed to be on a parallel decline along with the reports on evening news of race riots, threats of nuclear war with Cuba, and black kids being escorted by federal marshals to register in white universities, Teresa's family weathered the storms with apparent calm and reserve. Teresa stationed herself beside me in Mrs. Justice's third grade classroom from the first day of third grade onward. We learned spelling words, math problems and took recess together. Every moment not focused on books and our teacher during a school day, was focused on one another.

Teresa and I were two girls as engrossed in each others' thinking, breathing, talking, and moving as two separate humans could be. This is how we were for the next four years at Brutonville.

Teresa and I spent frequent weekends together either at her house in Troy or at mine down in the woods of Star. On one spring Friday of third grade, Teresa rode the bus home with me. She carried a speckled gray overnight case with everything that she would need for the weekend and the direction from her mother not to open the case until we were at home.

After dinner, Teresa and I went into the woods with ten-year-old Lee and six-year-old Dale leading the way. The woods were filled with dogwood trees bursting with white blossoms. Delicate green and yellow leaves covered the trees and joined together to make a forest of new smells and spackled softness all around. We walked and ran to our destination—the creek and the Tarzan vines.

The vines grew from the ground to the complete height of tall pines, oaks and maples and wrapped around the trees' trunks. We tore a vine loose from the ground and unraveled it part-way from the trunk, leaving it to dangle in the air. Lee yanked on the vine to test its ability to hold our weight. We took turns swinging from one side of the creek to the other, with much noise and physical commotion.

Teresa was intrigued by sixteen-month-old Frankie. Not yet solid on his feet, Frankie was a superior crawler. While Lee and Dale horsed around in our front yard at dusk, Frankie crawled from this thing to that, and Teresa and I played with the small dolls she had brought with her. My mother watched all of us from the top step of the front porch until she stood to go inside. "Keep an eye on Frankie," she said, but I was too busy with Teresa to give my brother attention.

Upon Mama's return to the top step with a smoldering cigarette wedged between her fore-finger and middle finger, she asked, "Where's Frankie?" Teresa and I scanned the yard. "Frankie!" Mama descended two of the four wooden steps. As she continued to call, Teresa and I moved closer to her. Soon we were all calling for my baby brother.

"He must be under the house!" Mama dropped to her knees and we children squatted beside her to peer into the blackness beneath the porch. "Is that him?" Mama pointed.

I heard my father's footsteps on the porch and the screen door slam closed behind him. The wooden joints creaked as he descended the steps. "Come here Frankie. Here! Here!" we called.

"God damn it. He's gonna get snake bit one of these days." Daddy paced back and forth like a mad bull behind us. "I don't know why the hell you don't watch him!" Daddy looked at my mother.

I knew about the danger of Frankie getting bitten by a snake or a black widow spider under the house because of what my parents said when he crawled under there a few times before. As my eyes adjusted to the darkness beneath the house, I could see my brother in the distance. He sat upright, head close to the floorboards of the house. This was typical of Frankie. He spent a lot to time just looking at you when you tried to get him to do or not to do something.

Mama said, "Somebody's got to crawl up under there and get him." Dale lunged onto his stomach and pulled himself over the dry, old-smelling soil. I looked at Teresa. Her eyes were bright and engaged in the commotion.

"Watch out for snakes." Mama yelled after Dale. Daddy walked to the woodpile and dug through the leftover scraps of construction lumber from his job. I watched Dale, and then I watched Daddy. Then I watched Dale again. Frankie was sitting still, neither moving away from Dale nor toward him.

Daddy found a quarter-inch thick, flat, slender piece of wood. He came back to the edge of the porch. "Get him out here." Daddy snapped the wood against denim covered legs–board against britches.

My stomach knotted. My breathing became ragged. "He don't know better Daddy." I tried to appeal to my father logically. Teresa's eyes widened as she watched my father flick the wooden paddle against himself.

"He's gotta learn." My stomach hurt and I felt as though I had to pee. I looked at my father's bigness. Frankie was small. I had already assessed that he did not learn a lesson by getting a punishment. One whipping about a thing is all it took for me, Lee or Dale to know a thing. In fact, it did not take more than words most of the time. But neither words nor spanking seemed to help Frankie learn. He had already been spanked once for going under the house. Daddy ranted on about Mama, how she was not doing her job and wondering just what good she was if she could not keep the child from going under the house.

Then Dale emerged with Frankie by the hand. In a flash Daddy had Frankie dangling in the air by one arm and paddled his behind with the board. Frankie cried loudly. I wanted to throw up. I could not stand the sight before my eyes.

Mama watched. She did not make Daddy stop. I hated her. *She is no good as a mama* I thought.

I scooped my crying Frankie from his seated, rubbing-his-wet-eyes position on the ground, into my arms. I ran with the weight of him bouncing with my stride. Teresa followed behind me calling my name and insisting, "Wait for me." Mama's calls to come back grew further and further away.

By the creek I found a log and snuggled down beside it with Frankie not crying anymore. Teresa stood over us breathing hard. I pulled Frankie against my chest. I rocked us and listened to the water moving around the rocks. I swore to God that I would do a better job of looking after my brother.

∞

Teresa's visits became less frequent over the subsequent years. I did not know then the great strain it put on my par-

94

ents to try to be normal–meaning to stay sober and not fight during her visits. That all of us children were growing older and still sharing one bed and a bedroom with our parents was not conducive to overnight company either.

But even though Teresa no longer visited me at my house after third grade, I continued to stay with her at her home at every opportunity during fourth, fifth and sixth grades. I, with a brown paper grocery bag filled with fresh pajamas, underwear and play clothes, was driven the twenty minutes out of Candor, through Biscoe and on to Troy, along with Teresa and her older brother and sister on many Fridays after school. A left turn at the county courthouse and we headed into the black section of Troy.

Teresa's family lived in a house sandwiched between Peabody, the black high school, and Mr. Anderson, Brutonville's principal's house. Her home had an inside bathroom, Teresa's bedroom was free of parents and brothers, they used a toaster to brown their sliced white bread in the morning, and her parents didn't drink and fight all weekend long. Being Teresa's best friend made me feel important, like I was someone special. I believed that I too gave Teresa something that was missing from her otherwise perfect world. I suspect I satiated her media-fed hunger for *whiteness*, as she sprinkled middle-class fairy dust over my poverty-ridden world. We were a perfect match, possessing each other's missing ingredient.

10

In May after the coolest days of spring were past, but before the full heat of summer, my brothers and I usually abandoned our shoes. The smooth surface of the black ground against my feet made me happy. It woke me up inside. It shook things around into their proper places. It made things right. Even when a blob of chicken poop squished between my toes, or if I cut my foot on glass or stumped my toe on a rock, I preferred no shoes.

Our bare-footedness bound my brothers and me to one another. We ran shoeless into the woods, over rain-softened dried leaves, through slow-flowing streams and over house-sized sawdust piles. We climbed trees in bare feet, followed narrow animal paths and traversed hot railroad tracks. We walked into town in our bare feet, and visited friends and relatives without our shoes.

But this wild abandon changed in the summer of 1964 when eleven-year-old Lee began donning socks and tennis sneakers. That summer he kept his feet dressed from sun up to sun down. It did not compute. How could he prefer the bondage of shoes to freedom? The summer was still the summer, the earth was the same cool ground, and we could have been unencumbered except for the presence of those canvas contraptions on my brother's feet.

"Why are you wearing tennis shoes?" I asked on the first day of summer break.

Irritated, he answered, "Because I want to."

"But why do you want to?"

"Because I do. Stop asking."

He was not only wearing shoes, I soon discovered, but was less interested in participating in our constant motion. He took to sitting on the couch and reading comic books. *Superman, the Fantastic Four, Spiderman, Archie.*

During the summer of 1964 he drew things. Rockets, dog's faces, and cars. Though he went into the woods with Dale and me sometimes, he became more interested in playing checkers or listening to the radio. Lee talked about musical groups that I did not know: *the Righteous Brothers, The Four Tops and Buddy Holly.* He became a stranger to me overnight. That summer I stood alone, by myself, flapping in the wind. The separation intensified the loneliness that Lee's involvement in my world kept at bay.

I turned more of my attention to two-and-a-half-year-old Frankie. I began bathing him, having him play the part of student as I played teacher. I tried to enjoy Dale but he was not the same as Lee. Dale needed someone to tell him what to do. Lee always already knew. I had lost my older brother to his friends at school before, but I had not experienced the odd kind of aimlessness that came from losing him while he was in our home with our family.

∞

As I stressed over the foreignness of Lee, I observed my parents as they watched the *Huntley and Brinkley* nightly news. The anchors brought word of northern college students going south to register black people to vote. At the time, I did not know I lived in the South. The name of our state was *North* Carolina after all. Mississippi, where the registration drive was happening, seemed to be a world away. In Star, we did not have police with guns and paddy wagons everywhere. That summer, churches were burned, gunshots were fired at innocent people and two white college boys and one black one went missing. The missing white boys caused people everywhere to get very upset about what was happening in Mississippi.

"That's something!" Mama said to Daddy. The living room was filled as usual with smoke from his L&M and her Salem cigarettes. "All those blacks been killed down there but, two missing white boys gets everybody's attention."

Huntley and Brinkley talked about the Civil Rights Bill. The bill meant school integration in the South and fair employment practices.

"J.F.'s paying the white fellas twice or three times as much as he pays me," Daddy said to Mama many times throughout the summer.

Things were getting shaken loose in my parents as they soaked in the news. In July, days after the report of President Johnson signing the Civil Rights Bill, we spotted Daddy's figure walking down the rocky road toward our house. Being on foot rather than driving J.F.'s red pickup at the end of the day grabbed all of our attention.

"Here comes Rob." Mama said with an *I wonder why he's walking* in her voice. Lee, Dale and I ran toward him.

"Daddy! Where's the truck?"

He did not smile as he did at the end of most work days. Being the big man that he was, his steps crunched on the rocks, his breath was deep and noisy. He carried the wrinkled brown paper bag that Mama put his lunch of biscuits and red eye ham in every morning. He carried a rusting thermos bottle by its handle. We didn't ask more questions as he did not answer the first one.

Mama flicked her Salem onto the ground from the porch and blew out her last long puff of smoke as Daddy and we climbed the steps. Inside the house, he sat down on the couch and let me unlace and remove his work boots. Mama watched.

"What happened?" she asked.

All we children stood up straight and watched Daddy's face. His eyes and mouth were drawn down at the edges. His voice when he spoke matched his eyes and mouth. "J.F. laid me off."

I wondered what *laid off* meant. "Why?" Mama asked as she pulled another Salem from the cigarette pack.

"Says not enough work."

"Anybody else laid off?"

"No."

Daddy pulled off his grayed athletic socks, dulled from hundreds of washings, and filled with smells of sweat and old-shoe insides. He stood from his chair. "We have to move."

Mama shook her head in a way that said *life is already hard and now it's going to get harder.* She walked into the kitchen and prepared dinner the same as every other weekday evening. My brothers and I played in the stilted angry way that children play when they are afraid of what is coming next in their lives and I began to grieve the loss of the home place that had come to mean everything to me.

11

The summer of 1964, Daddy began his new job at J.P. Morgan's sawmill. J.P., a white man who had lost half an arm at the elbow, loaned Daddy a truck to drive to and from work along with paying him wages.

Our new home was small and the sides were covered with light-blue-slate shingles. The house had three concrete steps at the entry of the front door. Some of the shingles were broken on the corners exposing the black tarpaper underneath. The blue boxy house was different from the one we had left.

Our former home was grayed by years of sunshine, wind, rain and snow. The old house had trees all around that hovered twice or three times as high as the house – a cedar tree, a giant oak, pines. The new house was absent porches, was surrounded by a bare yard and was also absent a well. The new house was in the black section of Star–in Dunn-Green Town. Dunn-Green Town was between the white section of Star and the Uwharrie National Forest.

Uwharrie spanned one hundred and seventy of Montgomery County's acres. The forest encompassed rolling hills, Indian burial grounds, sawdust piles, numerous streams and a river. Endless stands of oaks, pines, and cedars defined the landscape. The forest bordered Star to the south and Troy, the county seat, to the northwest. Forests similar to those that composed Uwharrie's surrounded Dunn-Green Town.

∞

Our new house was owned by one of the Greens who lived in New York City. They charged $13 a month for rent. Boyd Green, who lived a few houses away, collected the rent for his cousin and sent it to him through the mail each month.

Inside the new house was one long living room that spanned the entire width of the house. The living room had two parts separated by a wide doorless archway. One side of the room contained a wood stove and the other was empty. There were two bedrooms—one for my parents and one for us four children. There was a kitchen which was the same size of a bedroom. We did have an outhouse building at the new house, which I guess should have felt like an upgrade from doing your business out in the open. We had to go to the next door neighbor's well to draw water.

The new house was newer than our old house but it smelled acidic, like dried pee might smell on a warm, windy day. Later I learned that that smell was connected to the thriving world of cockroaches that lived beneath the house in the enclosed crawl space.

Our first night in the house, after the light had been turned off in the kitchen, we heard scratching noises. Upon turning the kitchen light on again, my father shouted "Goddamnit" which brought the rest of us crowding into the doorway.

My mother, three brothers, father and I stood transfixed watching hundreds of reddish cockroaches scamper to the edge of the table that we ate off, then onto and across the wall and behind the woodstove where they disappeared into cracks and openings in the tongue and groove wall paneling. Left behind were what seemed to be thousands of black specks and the strong acidic odor.

"Water bugs," Mama called them. My stomach turned as my nine-year-old mind imagined those little specks that the insects left behind in everything that I was to eat from that day forward. We had traded my paradise down in the woods for a house with a mass of roaches.

∞

In our new home's side yard, a fire burned within a circle of rocks. Seven kids and their parents from the two houses next to ours in Dunn-Green Town gathered around the fire. The adults sat in straight-backed chairs and on wooden logs looking at the fire.

Underneath the kitchen window hummed our electric freezer as it sat rusting from the North Carolina humidity and warm rains of the summer and cold ice freezes of the winter. Inside the freezer were bags of frozen string beans; strung, snapped, blanched and bagged for winter soups and suppers. Frozen bags of peeled and wedged peaches suspended in frozen sugar water would be used for pies, cobblers and fried peach turnovers. Pork chops, fatback and ribs from a slaughtered pig filled out the freezer.

The other children: Gloria, JoAnn, Bobo and Bumpie, along with my three brothers and I, stood around the fire holding sharpened sticks taken from pungent smelling wild bushes. Oscar Meyer wieners were stuck on the ends of the sticks.

I stood beside Gloria, who was closest to me in age of all the children but one year behind me at Brutonville Elementary. Gloria had a deep voice for an eight-year-old girl. We fanned smoke away from our faces and squirmed to the music coming from the radio atop the freezer.

(Hitch hike) Hitch hike, baby.

The kids held their franks over the fire and talked and laughed and paid attention to every one else's stick and frank. My parents and the other grownups laughed and talked and sipped their alcoholic beverages in the dimness of the light and in the fullness of our neighborliness.

Bernice, Gloria's aunt, was close to my mother's age. She raised Gloria's boy-cousin, Bumpie, alone. She spoke excitedly about her time in the big city of Charlotte.

"We went to clubs every night that I was there. And you should have seen all those soldiers! Dressed in camouflage uniforms with tight afros. They looked good enough to eat!" Mama, Bernice's sister, Chug, who lived with her at Gloria's grandparents' house, and another sister Cute, who lived in the house between mine and Gloria's, giggled while Daddy leaned forward and jabbed at the fire with a stick. Cute's husband leaned back in his chair with his arms folded over his chest.

We roasted until all the franks were gone and we were full

from hotdog sandwiches made of white buns, mayonnaise, mustard, catsup and onions. The freezer purred and we all grew quieter and softer. We buzzed from fun, food, drink and all our families together. I thought that the new place might not be so bad after all.

∞

That first summer in my new neighborhood, between fourth and fifth grades, I discovered one of my favorite places. Rhodie's juke joint down in the bottom. On a Saturday night my body jarred from feet stomping to Aretha Franklin's *Respect. Just a little bit.* And The King of Soul's *Papa's Got a Brand New Bag.* The small building, six inches off the ground, held twenty men, women and children. The twisting, grinding, turning, jumping, humping, tapping toes, and smacking shoes kicked up dust from the wooden floor.

Window sized openings in the walls let in the scant moving breezes from the warm night. People sweated and smiled and laughed and looked at each other in their eyes, at backs, at hips while snapping fingers, clapping hands, and bouncing shoulders. Beer was imbibed by the adults along with shots of liquor, sold by Rhodie's husband, from behind the plywood counter. Cigarettes were smoked and thumped out of the uncovered window openings.

Perfume applied for the evening, Tussy deodorant, and English Leather or Old Spice cologne mingled with the cigarette smoke and filled the air inside. Body scents, pure and bold, broke through too.

Outside the air was fresher. The sky was black overhead.

The Milky Way twinkled. Gloria's uncle Lee reminded us with a big smile on his face, "Don't count the Stars or you'll wake up with a casket beside your bed," Eyes quickly diverted from the heavens and took in the black shapes of trees and the kitchen lights at Mr. Boyd's house up the hill.

On Saturday nights, people overflowed with feelings of freedom and love. I let go of the weight of this thing and that thing and felt the hope that comes from being in the moment that you are in. A better day had arrived.

That was, until Mr. Boyd showed up and commanded loudly from the door of the joint, between the end of one song and the beginning of the next, that the place and the sinning inside had to go. "You people got to stop your drinking, your cussing and raising sand and get yourselves off to bed so that you are fit to meet the Lord on Sunday morning."

Rhodie eventually shut down the joint, but not before she built another one two times bigger out behind her own house, further from Mr. Boyd's place. Everyone seemed to sing and shout and praise the Lord right there at Rhodie's. It was where my neighbors from Dunn-Green Town and I let it all hang out.

12

On the first day of fifth grade in 1964, I, along with all the other black kids from Star rode Mr. James' bus through Biscoe and into Candor. Gloria, my new-found summer friend, went her way to fourth grade while I walked with Ola Mae, the only Star kid my age, toward our classroom.

Chunky Ola Mae and I had gone through first to fourth grades together at Brutonville Elementary. She lived on the other side of the hill in Dunn-Green Town. We had never been friends. Ola Mae's friends did not smile often; their eyes seemed dulled by things people never talked about in public.

When we reached Mr. Keith's fifth grade classroom door, that is where Ola Mae's and my connection to one another ended. She went to sit with her friends and I joined mine.

My best friend Teresa awaited my arrival. The moment our eyes met, we were in conversation about one another's lives. My school year had begun. Beverly, Deborah, Sharon, and the twins Avis and Javis joined Teresa and me.

"We went to Maryland this summer," Avis and Javis chimed out together.

"I went to New Jersey." Sharon spoke with a new maturity and sophistication.

"We should all choose boyfriends." I listened to Teresa and wondered which boy she had in mind to be hers; not knowing yet that she really meant, we should choose a pretend beau from our list of favorite celebrities.

Without responding to Sharon, the twins or Teresa, Beverly admired Deborah's necklace. "That is so pretty. Where did you get it?" I loved how the girls made enough noise to fill all the spaces between us.

"Good morning young men and women." A stocky, brown-skinned man with a well-groomed mustache, in necktie and suit stood before us. "It's time to take your seats so that we can begin our day." Mr. Keith had been Lee's teacher two years earlier. He did not take crap from any student. A boy that talked back to the teacher and did not do as he was told saw no second chances. Talking back warranted a palm slapping with a paddle. The more serious offenses of fighting at recess, or on the bus, or heaven forbid in class warranted a paddling. Mr. Keith's one by four inch, thick paddle was as long as a ten-year-old boy's arm.

I admired Mr. Keith. He dressed in a suit and tie every day to teach in front of thirty fifth graders. He loved math and loved for his students to love math. I had no idea how wonderful finding solutions to math problems could be. I learned about fraction and decimal multiplication. But it took concentration and effort. The other subjects that I had studied were easy to me. But math took my full attention.

During fifth grade, I shone in math, making A's all year for the first time ever.

Mr. Keith made me feel planted on the earth. He made me feel strong. His calm, consistent and firm approach to every-thing in a day glued me to the ground and kept me from floating off into worlds in my mind and beyond the win-dows of our pale yellow-walled school room. I did not spend my time thinking about Teresa and her pretend boyfriend, Elvis Presley, or dreaming about my pretend boyfriend, Guy Williams, the Cousin Will character from *Bonanza*. I spent time concentrating on the numbers printed on sheets of paper atop my letter-chiseled desk. Math gave me a feeling of efficacy, like dusting my mother's house. I could see the absoluteness of the answer, like the cleanness left after the dust was removed from a shelf or cabinet top. I loved math and the truth be known, I loved Mr. Keith too.

∞

Brutonville Elementary School felt like my home away from home by the time I reached sixth grade and eleven years of age. Over sixty children started first grade with me in 1960. Costella, Oletha, Eugene, Mike, Lorenza, Inez, Tabitha, Priscilla, Beverly, three sets of twins; Hilton and Milton, Avis & Javis, Martha and Patricia were some of my classmates' names.

Half of the kids traveled with me through Mrs. Hannah's second grade, Mrs. Justice's third, Mrs. Johnson's fourth, Mr. Keith's fifth into Mr. Spencer's sixth grade. Mr. Spencer wore the same suit and tie uniform as all the male teachers and principal at Brutonville. He was younger and hipper, though, than Mr. Keith. The girls in my class seemed to have a crush on Mr. Spencer. My allegiance stayed with Mr. Keith.

During sixth grade, Mr. Keith asked me to watch his fifth grade class whenever he had to be away for hours or for the day. I was not what you would call a substitute teacher because I did not teach. I was more a class monitor during his absence. I announced what pages the students were to work from over the period that we were to be together. I observed behavior, issued commands to be quiet and to focus on work, and I turned in names to Mr. Keith of those that failed to follow my directions. Getting your name turned in meant a whipping in front of the class with Mr. Keith's paddle. It was a deterrent for all but the most mis-behaved boys. Those same boys today might be diagnosed with some learning disorder and taught in a special class-room or by special teachers. But then, it was just misbehav-ing and punishment.

I excitedly waited through the hours before I was to attend the classroom of kids one year younger than I. Three neighbor kids from Dunn-Green Town–Gloria, Bobo and Gerce – were in Mr. Keith's class. I was interested in impressing them with my maturity.

In the wooden chair with arms, feet barely touching the floor and back barely touching the wood, I gave instructions from behind the old wooden desk. When quiet took over the room, my attention went to Mr. Keith's desk drawers. I developed a strategy for looking into them because I knew it to be wrong of me to ramble amongst his things. But back then, I had an irrepressible desire to search through boxes, drawers, cabinets and the like. They contained secrets and something about making a secret known, made me feel more secure.

For any kid witnessing, I looked about the top of the desk for something. I made all the expressions that one has when she cannot find a needed thing. And eureka, *The drawer. It could be there.* I thought these thoughts before pulling open the top drawer. Kids' things resided in that drawer, a paddle with ball attached by a rubber band, two yo-yos, a small pocket knife. Second drawer, long white envelopes and white paper, pens and pencils. Third drawer, a dictionary. I looked up words while the kids worked on their assignment.

When watching Mr. Keith's class, I felt the same mature feeling that I felt when I looked after my four-year-old brother Frankie. I was on my own. A group of people was listening to me and doing as I said. I felt powerful and smart and special for being the one asked to fill in for a teacher. I was thankful for Mr. Keith's attention and confidence in me. I would learn many years later that he wrote on my annual progress report that I was a natural leader. That is exactly how he treated me.

∞

Things came apart at Brutonville by the end of the 1965 – 66 school year. Desegregation laws forced black kids out of Brutonville and sent them to local white schools—the same schools my classmates and I had ridden past on our yellow bus every school day of the previous six years. Near the end of sixth grade, the erosion of my tight cohort commenced.

"We're moving to Concord. I won't be coming back to Brutonville next year." Teresa wore a serious look on her face as she shared with us the plans for her future.

"What?" I felt my breath quicken and my chest fill with emotion.

"You're going where?" Avis asked.

"I know." Teresa assured me with the expression on her face. "Mama got a new job and we're moving."

"She won't be teaching at Brutonville next year?" Deborah clarified.

"No."

"Dang," Avis said. "Why y'all movin'?"

"Brutonville won't need as many teachers anymore." Avis, Deborah, Beverly, Teresa and I looked at one another with shocked and quizzical expressions on our faces. We all knew of desegregation. Some of the kids had already gone on to the white schools closest to their homes. But the girls in my group of friends had not spoken to one another about what the southern school integration plan meant, or would mean to us. For that moment, desegregation took on the meaning of heartbreak. I wondered how I was going to exist without my best friend. Sixth grade would be our last year together.

∞

Teresa's impending departure unhinged something in me. The security I had come to know from riding Mr. James' bus from Star, through Biscoe, into Candor to Brutonville for six years diminished. The warmth I felt for the cafeteria women that had served me oatmeal and milk in the morning and a lunch of meat, starch and vegetable every school day for nine months out of each of the previous six years became blunted. The bond between me and the other kids was cracked. My dreams of having one teacher or another in my upper grades evaporated like mist in the sun.

The vulnerability that I felt over Teresa's leaving worked itself into my being and zapped the confidence that had become my inseparable school companion. My sense of belonging became rattled. For the first time in years, the whiteness of my skin seemed to matter in relation to where I was supposed to belong.

∞

A few days after Teresa's news, two years earlier than was mandated for us to desegregate, I elected to go to Star's white elementary school for seventh grade. The unease born out of losing a best friend made me want to strike out on some path of my own. I fixed on the future, on moving forward, rather than feel the pain of loss and the insanity of what was out of my control.

∞

On the last day of the sixth grade before leaving Mr. Spencer's classroom, I said goodbye to Teresa. She, I, and the other girls stood in a huddle and talked. "I'll write to y'all and y'all write me. Okay?" Teresa directed.

"Okay," we all promised.

"And I guess I'll see y'all in high school." I addressed Avis, Deborah and Beverly as they looked back at me blankly. Maybe they were contemplating their own futures away from Brutonville. I turned and walked away from the girls, most of whom had shared my school life since first grade. I felt awkward and tried to picture a new best friend at Star Elementary.

My body tightened like a rubber band being stretched as I walked toward the bus. My surroundings changed from the inside of Mr. Spencer's classroom and my school friends to the sidewalk that led to the buses lined up to take us to different towns. Darker skinned kids, my age and younger, swarmed around me on their way to their buses, all squealing and talking about the last day of school.

I glanced back at the cafeteria building that housed the small library. I looked toward the classrooms where upper classmen went to school. I looked at the playground where I had ridden on the merry-go-round since before I turned six years old. I walked past Ola Mae as she walked in the same direction and reached Gloria and Gerce. My focus moved from my classmates and Brutonville to my summer companions from the Star community. *I can't wait until next year* I thought to myself when *I'll have a brand new set of friends.* I held my head high, chin up, smiled, the way I did when I didn't want anyone to know about the fear, the pain, or the sadness inside me.

13

My older brother Lee, at age thirteen, on the anniversary of his completing elementary school and preparing for high school, was determined that he was going to wear his hair long in the African bush style. By the summer of 1966, afros were the rage and Lee's curly black crop was starting to take the rounded shape of young men's on *American Bandstand* and *Soul Train*. But Daddy was determined that no son of his was going to look so unkempt.

"I'm taking you and Dale for haircuts. Come on." Daddy spoke to Lee as he walked through our house searching for the railroad cap that he was going to use to cover his baldness.

"I don't want a haircut." I listened from my position in front of the family's mirror as Lee reasoned that he should be able to grow his hair if he wanted.

"You're gonna get a haircut." Dale and Mama also watched Lee and my father as their interchange became louder. Lee's direct assertiveness was not common. I stiffened and stopped arranging my own hair.

"I'm not." Lee stood from his seated position.

"You get your ass out there in that truck now. You too Dale," he motioned for Dale to move it.

Mama hummed under her breath, paced and retrieved tossed pieces of children's clothing from the backs of chairs. I became transfixed by Lee's body language. He was standing steady on both feet looking square at Daddy.

"No."

Our fifty-four-year-old father stepped toward him. Lee lifted the caned-bottom chair from the floor next to him. Daddy stopped.

"No son of mine is going to be walking around looking like a jigger boo."

"It's my hair."

The two went on for several more interchanges, swaying, eyes locked, Lee holding the chair between himself and our father. Then to my relief, Daddy walked away.

"Get in the truck," he said to Dale and walked out of the house without another word. Before that day, I did not know that a child of my father's could stand up to him and impose their will. I felt an inkling of power stir within me.

∞

The time of *sap's rising* was when the summer heat and humidity hit us in the face and squeezed our bodies until we burst with the venom formed like oil from the pressing of old rotting stuff within the earth. We spewed out a "No," we gave the evil eye, we said "Leave me alone, now, I ain't playing." We said these type words more times and to many more people than we would have in the spring, the fall or

118

even in a cold, bitter winter. Nobody could escape the sap's rising in our little community of black folks.

One summer evening during this period of discontent in my eleventh year, I along with Gloria and Gerce observed Gloria's Aunt. Bernice, a single woman of thirty-something who had never married, lived with her parents, Gloria's grandparents, and with Bernice's son—Gloria's cousin Bumpie.

"I don't take no shit from no man," she told us girl children as she drew a dark line along her lower eyelid with an eyeliner pencil. She continued, "I'm gettin' ready for something good tonight girls." She laughed and lifted her breasts as she swayed her narrow hips from side to side in the slinky gold-colored dress that stopped halfway between her hips and knees. She watched us watching her and laughed, which made us laugh with her.

Bernice pulled at swirls of hair that were gleaming from being straightened with Royal Crown grease and a hot comb. She arranged her bangs on her forehead and shaped the rest of her hair with a five-pronged hair pick. We watched and I soaked in every bit of Bernice's shimmering dress, dangling earrings and matching gold heels. "Those soldier boys won't know what hit them when they see me coming through the door!"

Bernice was bold. She was going out to the clubs and was planning to take my mama with her. Gloria, Gerce and I followed her as she walked the rock-covered path layered with cracked quartz atop hard red earth. Twenty feet from my back door, Bernice yelled.

"Ovella, Vella. You coming?"

Daddy stepped into the back door opening. "She ain't going nowhere."

"Why not?" Bernice put her hands on her hips in her top sassy form.

"Not your business why. She ain't going."

Bernice looked past my Daddy into the door of our kitchen and yelled over and past him. "'Vella. Honey. Come on. You don't have to listen to him."

Daddy stepped down the cinder block step and took Bernice's arm. It was something I had never seen him do, touch a woman outside of our family. "Go on now. Git on home. She ain't going."

"Don't you touch me, Mister!" Bernice jerked her arm out of Daddy's hand. "I don't play that game. No sir."

Daddy pushed Bernice at that point and as she stumbled backwards, he kicked gravel at her, the way you might at an aggressive dog. "G'won home now. Ain't gonna tell you again."

Bernice exploded. "You fucking son-of-a-bitch. You don't tell this woman what to do. I'll fucking kill you!"

The dust started rising around my father and Bernice from their foot motion. Daddy took Bernice by the arm again and swung her around. Her ankles twisted in the high heels, her skirt shifted upwards, her upper body leaned forward. I fanned at the dust. My throat felt gritty.

And down Bernice went onto the ground. I was speechless. In the shock of the moment, I could no longer hear though I saw Gloria and Gerce's mouths moving and their hands touching their faces. Bernice was on the ground in her gold dress, with her hard pressed hair moving, one stocking at the knee ripped, blood on the kneecap. She scrambled up and pushed at my father. He pushed back. Mama yelled from the back door. "Just go Bernice."

"I don't take this shit!" Bernice shot back at my mother. "I'll kill the mother fucker!" Before Bernice turned to go home, she spat at Daddy. Gloria and Gerce chattered animatedly back and forth to one another as they followed her down the path.

I stood stone petrified as Daddy walked toward the back door. My mind and my body filled with dread. I turned and walked around the house to the barren front yard. Through the shock, I reflected on the craziness of the previous moments and my father's role in it.

∞

It was late before my family all went to bed the Saturday night after Daddy's fight with Bernice. My parents slept in one double sized bed in one bedroom and my three brothers and I slept in the second bedroom on the other side of the wall from theirs. My brothers' and my beds were iron framed models, with tall ironwork headboards and foot rails.

Our mattresses rested atop a palette of linked metal pieces. The palette of metal was no longer as tight as it once was. It sagged in the middle which meant that the cotton and spring mattresses also sagged in the middle. Thirteen-year-old Lee and nine-year-old Dale slept in one bed and five-year-old Frankie and I slept in the other. The two beds sat two feet apart and filled the entire room except for a narrow path to and from the door.

The air was stale and humid in the dark bedroom where my brothers and I slept although the window was wide open. I punched a flat pillow and lay without a cover upon me. "Get over," Lee commanded Dale from the other bed. I looked at Frankie, already sleeping.

As I drifted into sleep, I was reawakened by the sound of my parents' bed. The exposed rusty metal rings of their spring mattress were thick. The springs that we jumped on and propelled ourselves into the air from when they were not at home creaked and groaned and mingled with their human grunts and moans.

My eyes flapped open to our bedroom's darkness. I quieted my startled breathing and my own movement while my eyes adjusted to the blackness of the room. More groans and bed spring squeaking. I froze. What was happening? I suspected that my father was hurting my mother. I recalled the time when he choked her against the refrigerator. I listened through the darkness for signs of the outcome of their bed altercation. I wrestled within my own mind to disentangle his voice, his sounds from hers. I felt uncomfortable, vulnerable in the room with my brothers. I wondered if they listened too. I wanted to disappear. I had no success in figuring out which sounds belonged to whom or how much damage was being done.

I listened a long time beyond the cessation of noise for signs that my mother was still alive. I heard the familiar sound of my fathers' snoring. I feared what sight might greet my eyes in the light of morning. Thinking and dreaming that your father has killed your mother in the bedroom next to you wears on your physical strength. I knew for sure that night that if my arms were wings, I would have flown out of that house and not ever returned.

14

I awoke early on Sunday morning to the sound of my father's work-booted feet on our living room floor. I registered the feeling of having had a nightmare. Then I recalled that it was not a dream. I remembered the previous night's fears about my mother's safety. I listened for her steps or voice. I dressed myself and exited the bedroom, leaving my brothers as they stretched and argued with one another.

Daddy seemed in a pleasant mood as he often was the morning after a bad day and night. I did not feel happy toward him.

"Hey," I said to Daddy as I looked at the bedroom door wherein my mother still lay. I thought to myself that he was in much too good a mood to have awakened beside a dead woman. This thought brought some comfort. I pushed their bedroom door open and peeked inside. There sat Mama on the edge of her bed. She did not see me peering in. I pulled the door to and thought about how happy I was to see her alive.

For the remainder of the morning, while I folded the line-dried laundry that had been left spread on the living room couch the previous two days, I dreamed of driving a Volkswagen Beetle with flowers painted all over it, out of my neighborhood and out of Star. I imagined what it might be like to be a movie star in Hollywood.

The job of folding laundry did not take much thought and left lots of room for thinking and dreaming. Mama clacked around our house in brown sandals and a blue house dress. My father tromped back and forth from their bedroom past me—probably engaged in slipping sips of the white lightning hidden either in a clothes drawer, the old wardrobe, or in the bottom of the bureau.

My brothers busied themselves with their usual weekend morning chores. Lee filled the three buckets of water from the neighbor's well. Dale carried out half-gallon mason jars filled to the brim with pee from everyone's night-time bladder evacuations.

My baby brother, Frankie, who was four and half and mentally slow because he had been premature at birth, laughed and zipped in and out of the wide open front door.

Frankie was small for his age. He was beautiful with golden tanned skin and freckles on his face so large and plentiful that he looked dirty. His curly black hair fit with his nose, lips and eyes just so to make a perfect face. Everyone loved Frankie even though he was always getting himself into trouble. He did not get the lesson from punishments, so he repeated the offense over and over, eliciting the same punishment of a spanking over and over from my father, which I tried to prevent at every opportunity. Every pain of Frankie's had always been my pain too.

With my family busy doing morning things, Mr. Boyd,

our neighborhood's most holy deacon, paid Mama and Daddy a visit. The deacon stood tall on the front door step, hat in his hand, Sunday-church suit and tie on, and knocked on the wooden door frame that shaped the opening into our house. "How y'all today Mister, Misrus Gaddy?" His voice preceded him into our house. He had a definite presence about him.

After polite exchanges and commenting to my parents, "Your boys sure are growing into fine young men," he got to the business he had come about. "I stopped by Mrs. Richardson's uptown there the other week and found her out cold on the floor in her living room. Turned out she had a gall bladder attack."

Mama and Daddy said a few "Don't says," before Mr. Boyd continued.

"She's back home now. Went down to Pinehurst and got a operation. Her childrens concerned 'bout her falling out again and nobody bein' 'round to help her." My parents nodded their heads. "She needs somebody to look out for her while she recuperates."

From the couch, I followed the conversation closely, as I did all conversations coming in through our front door for my parents, or my brothers for that matter.

"I was thinking about your girl there," Mr. Boyd tipped his head toward me. "I seen how good she is at takin' care of your youngest." My parents looked my way and nodded in agreement. I felt my breath quicken and my eyes widen. I am sure my expression told my parents of my interest in the proposition being put before them.

I culled from the rest of the deacon's and my parents' conversation that Iola Richardson was a rich white woman who was a bit peculiar. She was known for being stingy, most likely due to living through the Depression, my parents and Mr. Boyd surmised. She refused to tell people her age. She pretended she was not working in the yard by tossing down a rake she might be using when folks drove by her house. She wanted no witnesses to her act of gathering leaves, thus ruling out a chance of someone's call to one of her children about her being out taxing herself unnecessarily.

Near the conclusion of Mama and Daddy's conversation with Mr. Boyd, my mother asked me what I thought. "I want to help her out." I stood from my seated position on the couch. "When can I start?"

Mr. Boyd said that he would let Mrs. Richardson know we would be coming by. I folded the remaining clothes. Within minutes I had a large brown-paper grocery bag and was in the bedroom packing three pairs of shorts and four shirts, my Sunday dress, seven pairs of multicolored nylon underwear with the days of the week printed on them, and a pair of baby doll pajamas that were too small for me. After placing my clothes in the bag, I looked around the bedroom that I shared with my three brothers.

The room smelled of boys sweaty socks mingled with pee. I looked at the bed that Frankie and I shared. One torn sheet placed over a sagging mattress. Lee and Dale's bed also sagged and was the source of the pee odor. Dale had been a bed wetter a good six of his nine years of living. *I will not miss this place* I said to myself.

With the ease in which it was all happening, somebody might have thought that my parents and I had been planning for the occasion of my leaving home to work at age eleven since the day I was born. It was no secret to my family that I thought our four-room house with six people, of whom all were males except for me and my mama, was way too small. It was no secret to me that my parents thought me and my brothers were getting too old to all be sleeping in the same room. My father having left home and gone to work at age eleven paved the way for the experience to seem a normal one for a family to have.

∞

"What you got there?" Mama pointed at the brown bag I carried as we departed from our house on the Monday evening following Mr. Boyd's visit.

"My clothes."

"How do you know you're gonna need clothes? You don't know if she'll want you to stay."

I didn't answer my mother. I climbed into my father's borrowed pickup truck and held the bag in my lap. I felt happy to be leaving our house. I wouldn't have to squirm every time I saw a neighbor looking at Mama when she was sloppy drunk. I wouldn't have to witness my daddy beating on the neighbor women or my mother. I wouldn't have to worry if Mama made it alive through the night. I did however feel the slightest guilt and much sadness when I waved goodbye to Frankie. He stood on the doorstep watching us pull out with a *Where-you-going-without-me?* look on his face.

The seven-minute-drive from my neighborhood, over the

railroad track, past Dr. Scarborough's house with acres of land that included his own woods, into the white section of Star on the main road, ended in front of Iola Richardson's place. When we pulled into her driveway, my eyes filled with the vision of her home and property. I took in the sights while Daddy emptied his sinuses into his red bandana handkerchief, making the usual sound of coal being poured down a metal shoot. Mama puffed the last few draws on her cigarette before smashing out it's fire in the truck's overflowing ashtray.

I admired Mrs. Richardson's soft yellow house with awnings over all the windows. I admired the grass-covered ground, the neat height of the lawn, the abundant trees, bushes and shrubs. There were flowers of what seemed every possible color. An American flag hung by Mrs. Richardson's front door fluttering in the breeze.

I climbed out of the truck behind my mother.

"Leave that bag!"

I put the bag of clothes back on the seat of the truck and followed my parents down the paved driveway. My eyes were pleased by the order of things. There was not one spot of browned grass or rocks piled on patches of bare earth. A bush taller than me with the loveliest smelling white flowers, sat to the side of the brick colored carport which sheltered the most beautiful old turquoise and white Chrysler Saratoga automobile.

My lungs filled with the delicious aroma of the plant Mama called "Gardenia." Before Iola Richardson came to the door, I reached out and touched the white blossom. The petals were soft, thick, and full of the sweet smell. I put my fingers to my nose. The fragrance mingled with the smell of my parents' cigarette smoke. *Gardenia* I said to myself over and over. I was carried away with the silky smooth dreams of a prince charming-like character that a gardenia can make an eleven-year-old girl have.

And there she stood at the door. Old. Grey haired. Grey glasses covered grey eyes. Wrinkled creamy white skin with rouged red cheeks. The woman stood soundly, and when the time came, moved briskly. Her voice was solid, no nonsense.

"Hello. Come in." She held the screened door open for us. We, one by one, moved past the woman. I could guess what she was thinking from seeing my dark-featured father and my tanned, brown-eyed mama, then me, looking every bit like I did not match them with my freckled white skin, brown hair straight compared to theirs, and green eyes. I looked at her face and smiled as I passed. She smelled of perfume. She smiled back at me.

Inside I scanned windows draped with white lacy curtains, an organ with sheet music positioned ready to be played, and an arched entry into a dining room with eight chairs around a long table. Mrs. Richardson's living room, my father looked like a giant in his white t-shirt and blue overalls. I looked at his work boots; dusty, paint speckled and cracked atop the tan-colored carpet. He stood with his railroad cap in his hand. An indentation in the skin was left where the cap had pressed.

Mama looked small beside him and rough against the

neatness of the house. Her hair looked frizzy and tousled. She wore a polyester dress that would have been much better had she worn stockings and nice shoes, instead of showing scarred legs and sporting black loafers with cheap shiny buckles and dust in the crevasses where the shoes were sewn together. We all looked at the couch and chairs. Their absolute cleanness must have been what made us remain standing. My mind became saturated with honeyed thoughts of living in the house with all its softness, its sweet smells, and the lively old woman.

"And your name is?" Mrs. Richardson looked at me.

"Levonne." My parents and Mrs. Richardson talked about specifics of an arrangement while I continued to take in the surroundings.

"I'll show you where she'll stay." Mrs. Richardson led us out of the living room through the dining room and into a kitchen with a shiny dark-green tiled floor, cabinets on two walls and a large two-part sink sunken into a dark green counter. To one side of the kitchen sat a glass-topped table with four chairs around it. The fragrance of baked bread lingered in the air. My stomach growled.

My bedroom was separated from the rest of the house and had its own entrance to the outside. Mrs. Richardson explained that the room had been a back porch that she had converted into an art room and now it would be used as the bedroom for the live-in help.

The room was bright with windows on three sides. A twin bed sat beneath one set of the windows. A larger bed sat beneath the windows on the opposite side of the room. Iola Richardson asked, "When can she start?"

I blurted out, "I have my clothes with me."

My parents looked embarrassed but Mrs. Richardson said, "Good, then. You can settle in now?"

It felt awkward standing in a stranger's driveway with a person I had just met, waving goodbye to my parents and knowing I would not be going home that night. It felt exciting too as it had felt when my brothers and I were younger and had just begun school or had started out to explore the woods. Living with and working for Iola Richardson was going to be an adventure.

∞

I took my first shower at Mrs. Richardson's house. After my parents left, she showed me the bathroom. She said, "Why don't you take a nice shower and wash that curly hair of yours." She told me to use the beige towels because she saved the flowery ones for company.

"Yes ma'am."

"Your parents are doing you a real service by teaching you good manners," she said. "Too many children don't know good manners anymore. I must say that is one good thing colored people do for their children." Mrs. Richardson touched the light switch. "Now be sure to turn the lights off after you're finished. Electricity costs money and money doesn't grow on trees."

I nodded my head and said, "Yes ma'am" as I recalled that Iola Richardson lived through the Great Depression thus making her stingy about money.

"Try not to use too much hot water. And when you're finished, take the Comet there and the sponge to clean the tub." On her way out, her arm brushed against mine. She was softer than I thought she would be.

I shimmied out of my shorts and shirt and stepped into the bathtub. The curtain hanging there from the rod to the bottom of the tub looked much too nice to get dirty from a shower, so I put it outside of the tub to be sure not to splash shampoo and soap all over it. I turned the hot water on, keeping it weak like Mrs. Richardson told me to do, and then I added the cold.

When the water was just right, I closed my eyes and turned my face toward the shower spout as people in T.V. soap commercials did. I reached down and turned the knob redirecting the water. In the pipes, there was a sputtering sound as it traveled through to the spout. I couldn't wait and there it came! Cold as ice! I coughed and spit and stumbled back away from the water. It went up my nose and didn't feel a thing like the people looked in commercials.

Mrs. Richardson's bedroom was next to the bathroom. She called to me to see if I was all right. I said "Yes ma'am. I'm alright." I reached out my hand to find the stream of water warm enough to resume my shower, this time with my face down to keep from drowning myself.

I guess I stayed a little long in the shower because just when I was getting ready to rinse the pretty smelling shampoo out of my hair, Mrs. Richardson knocked on the door and said, "Hurry up now. You've been long enough." So I rinsed my hair and exited the shower.

When Mrs. Richardson told me later that the pretty curtain on the silver rod in the bathroom was made for getting wet, instead of the floor, I was a bit embarrassed seeing as what she said made common sense. I always put the shower curtain inside the tub from that time forward.

∞

The first evening at Mrs. Richardson's was fun. I sat with her in her bedroom as though we'd done the routine many times before. The bench, scooted out from beneath her makeup table, was my seat. She sat propped with several pillows in her bed, a sweater draped over her night-gowned shoulders, sipping on a glass of Mogen David wine.

"Don't say a word to anyone about my drinking this. The doctor said I should take it every night to help with my varicose veins." I was used to seeing people drink all kinds of beer and liquor. None of them ever apologized or seemed the least bit ashamed. I liked that she cared.

At nine o'clock on the dot, the television was off and it was bedtime. I had always looked forward to bedtime. Whereas most kids I knew thought it was great to stay up as late as possible at night, I looked forward to getting to bed so I could tune into my dreams. Sometimes I tried to program the dreams when there was something I wanted to experience like getting a particular toy for Christmas or being with friends on May Day at school or having a special movie star boyfriend.

On my way to bed the first night at Mrs. Richardson's house, I reflected on how I had spent most of my life sleeping either with my whole family in one room or with my brothers. *Now I have a bedroom to myself,* I thought. It felt luxurious to stop at the inside bathroom to pee instead of going outside to a toilet or peeing in a jar. On through the dining room, into the kitchen I had thought, *I'll get a glass of water and put it by my bed.* Mrs. Richardson had put a glass of water by her bed in case she became thirsty in the night. So that is what I did.

My new bed was the twin bed. It did not sag in the middle. I pulled back the top cover to expose a light-weight blanket and a top sheet. The top sheet was most exciting as at my parents' house, it was one sheet per bed and the sheets most likely were torn in a place where your hand or foot got caught, making the hole bigger.

I sat down, lifted my feet off the floor and slid myself between the sheets. *Glorious* I thought. The fresh fragrance of clean bed linens filled my nose. I laid my head on a fluffy pillow. My pillow at home didn't have a pillow case on it and was so flattened there was no fluff left.

There I lay, on my back, looking out of a big window at the stars beyond the tree tops. *Glorious* I thought again. That night I wanted to dream about living in a beautiful house with flowers all around and having a loving grandmother. Sometimes the programming worked and sometimes it didn't. The softness of the bed and the quietness of the room embraced me as I drifted off into a sleep filled with dreams about being chased by bad people and my legs not working properly. *How on earth could such a perfect day end with such panicky dreams?* It did not occur to me at the time that on some level, a child of eleven must have some anxiety about leaving home.

∞

The next week, on the first Saturday night at Mrs. Richardson's, we watched her favorite show. *Lawrence Welk* had never been a favorite of mine, but she ate it up. The regular black person on the show was Arthur Duncan doing his tap dancing, which was boring to me. I had no idea that before long, I would be enjoying right along with Mrs. Richardson , watching Jo Ann Castle playing the piano like she didn't care if she tore it into pieces with her banging and the Lennon Sisters with their sweet melodies.

When my first Sunday at Mrs. Richardson's came, I felt disappointed and lonely from her leaving me while she went off to her white folk's Methodist Church. I had supposed that she would take me with her. After all, my Sunday church dress was ready for wearing, and I was accustomed to going to Green Grove United Church of God back home whenever I felt like it. Instead she told me, "You stay here. I'll be gone for only a few hours. You can watch the television if you like."

Rocky and Bullwinkle, Mr. Magoo, the Reverend Billy Graham Jr.'s sermon. Part of the morning I smiled at the antics of cartoon characters. The rest of the time I tuned into the Rev. Graham talking about how to repent my sins and be saved in three easy steps. I also took the chance to check out Mrs. Richardson's house more thoroughly.

I looked through her closets. Sets of matching skirts and tops made of heavy, thick cloth in varied shades of peach, brown and cream hung on wooden hangers in her bedroom closet. The suits felt coarse to my touch. The material was not the thin, lightweight material as the dresses my mother wore. I examined Mrs. Richardson's pump-style shoes lined on the floor of the closet. I counted nine pairs.

I pushed far back into the rear of the closet to find tins of various shapes and sizes stacked in a pile. I explored the contents of each tin. Some were empty but two contained treats. Danish butter cookies and chocolate covered cherries. I could not resist tasting samples of each. The cookies melted in my mouth and tasted every bit as delicious as they smelled. The chocolate covered cherries made my taste buds burst alive upon contact with the cherry flavored syrup and creamy white filling. The chocolates and cookies were most luxurious compared to the hard whorehound candies my brothers and I filched from my father's clothing drawer.

After the treats, I examined the perfume bottles on Mrs. Richardson's dressing table. I felt the ridged designs of the bottles, sniffed their caps, and read the names. I spelled and pronounced each one out loud as if I were going to be tested. C-h-a-n-e-l-N-o-.-5. *Chanel Number Five.*

Inside the top drawer of her dresser were thick incandescent necklaces, matching earrings, broaches and bracelets. I held a pearl necklace in my hands and imagined how I would look in it with a touch of Iola Richardson's rouge on my face. I fastened the pearls around my neck, then reached for the compact with the rouge in it. At the very moment of reaching, I heard the Saratoga's engine. I took the necklace off and placed it in the drawer. I turned off the television and ran back to my room in time for Mrs. Richardson to find me lying on my bed instead of rambling through her things.

∞

By dinner time on Sunday, we were soft and cozy from sitting around all afternoon and taking it easy in the North Carolina humidity and heat. After dinner, Mrs. Richardson played songs on her organ and had me sing along. "Mexicali Rose" and "My Wild Irish Rose" were songs I had never heard before but ones whose tunes I loved. By the same time on Sunday evening at my parents' house, my brothers and I would have been in a state of post traumatic stress from living with Mama and Daddy and their drinking and fighting all weekend.

∞

Mrs. Richardson had a basement with a washer and a dryer. It was my job to do the laundry. She showed me the amount of detergent to be put into the washer and where to put the settings. She gave strict instructions on not mingling my clothing with other of the household items or with hers.

I thought the instructions about *not* mingling to be a bit odd as my mother always mingled all of our family's clothing together on laundry day. But nonetheless, the first time that I washed the clothes on my own, I planned to follow the instructions.

After placing the clothes in the washer, while still there in the basement, I searched through shelves of old books and magazines. The books that my family had at home were an old set of *Encyclopedia Britannicas*. One by one, I flipped through pages of *Look* magazines and *National Geographics*.

Though the musty mold smells made my eyes tear and my nose itch, I loved looking at the *National Geographic's* spectacular color pictures of far away people and places. It was the first time I had seen pictures of dark people in Africa with painted naked bodies. I was mesmerized by the sight. I had previously thought *Jujus* in the Tarzan movies to be made up. There were other pictures of all kinds of wonderful things. Beautiful tigers, penguins in the Antarctic, whales, gorillas, people living in the Andes that wore brightly colored clothes and funny derbies on their heads.

In the midst of my imaginary expedition, Mrs. Richardson interrupted. "What? Not finished yet?" She seemed irritated.

I was so engrossed in my adventure of discovery that I forgot to put clothes from the washer into the dryer and to start the next load. I apologized and snapped to attending the chore. I shoved clothing from the washer into the dryer as I had observed my mother do multitudes of times in the public pay laundromat. Then I gathered the remaining two small piles of soiled laundry and filled the washing machine. "Wait now." Mrs. Richardson touched my arm. "I told you not to mingle your things with the other things."

I was aware of putting my clothes in the washer with hers, but it seemed a logical decision as I hurried to get on with my task. The washer had been only half full with the one pile. It made sense to fill the machine. *The combining will save on electricity* I thought.

But before I could say a word to explain the logic of my actions, Mrs. Richardson ordered, "Take those things out." She pointed at a piece of my clothing. I imagined my things must stink as I removed one by one, a shirt, a pair of underpants, a pair of shorts. "You can't have those things in there with the dish towels." As Mrs. Richardson was emphatic on the matter, I removed the remainder of my things. I wondered to myself *how much dirtier my bottom must be than hers. She mingles her underwear with the kitchen linen.*

I kept close tabs on the remainder of the laundry. But before the work was complete, I discovered bottles of Coca Cola and Fresca in the basement's refrigerator. But no matter how much I enjoyed the refreshing flavor of the lemony drink and the *National Geographics*, I could not shake the oddness of Mrs. Richardson's insistence on each person's clothing being washed separate from the other.

∞

To make it quicker and easier for me to run errands to the grocery and drug stores, Mrs. Richardson gave me a shiny new blue bicycle. My brothers and the other boys in the old neighborhood had bicycles, but girls did not have them.

The first time I rode my bicycle back to my parents' home, all the children looked my way, pointed their fingers and waved excitedly. As I approached them, I stood on my pedals and glided past like a swan on a lake.

At my parents' home, I chattered at anyone who would listen about what I was getting and doing at Mrs. Richardson's. "I have my own bedroom. I take showers in an indoor bathroom. I have my own towels, my own tube of toothpaste, new pajamas, new shoes, a new yellow dress for when we go visiting her friends and best of all," I told my parents. "I have a top sheet *and* a bottom sheet on the bed where I sleep."

My father made no comment, but Mama let out a strong "*humph*," shook her head, and walked away from me without saying a word. My excitement over Mrs. Richardson's things did not bring my mother closer to me. At the time, I didn't understand how my mother could let me go off to live with a rich person and disapprove at the same time.

∞

Later in the summer, Mrs. Richardson decided to take a trip to Florida to see her daughter and adopted granddaughter who was my age. I wondered if Mrs. Richardson might adopt me after hearing how her daughter and son-in-law raised their adopted child into the pretty, curly haired girl whose picture hung on the wall of Mrs. Richardson's guest bedroom.

But I was not invited to go along on the trip, which meant going back home. I had become accustomed to an inside bathroom, to sleeping in my own room and to the peace and quiet of a sane family life, so I was disappointed to have to go back to my parents' house to stay while Mrs. Richardson took a trip.

∞

Back home, after interacting with my family, I went to my friend Gloria's house where I watched her straighten her hair while I tuned in and out of her grandma and aunt's conversation about the colored people in Watts, California gone mad rioting and destroying their own neighborhood.

Gloria applied Royal Crown hair dressing to small sections of hair before raking the hot metal comb through, transforming spongy-looking, puffy bunches into shiny straight black locks. After she rolled the last section of straightened hair onto a pink sponge roller, we walked to the playground behind Gloria's house. Most all of the children in the neighborhood were getting too old to play on the sliding board or the big three person swing. But most of us liked to sit at the picnic table on the edge of the playground, surrounded by no house too close by, and talk about whatever was important to us.

∞

The week at home ended and I was back at Mrs. Richardson's with Mama's old yellow and black straw-textured suitcase laid out on my bed. Mrs. Richardson stood talking about wonderful things she had seen and done in Florida while I unpacked. A movement on my bed caught my and her eye at the same time. A water bug scampered across the bedspread.

"Oh my god! You brought one of those cockroaches back up here!" Mrs. Richardson jumped back and began looking for something with which to hit the bug. "Don't let it get away." I herded the bug into the middle of the bed while she grabbed a broom. She swatted the bug and made me take my suitcase outside in case I'd brought more of the little creatures back with me. She said, "Once they get started in a place, it's very hard to get rid of them." She also said, "Filth and dampness make those nasty things flourish."

Now I wouldn't call my mama's house filthy, though it could use better care. Mama's philosophy was *why clean up when four wild youngins are just going to mess it right back up?* Though my mother might have been partially right, that water bug embarrassed me. I shook every piece of clothing and banged the suitcase hard on the landing outside my door before reentering. I cringed when Mrs. Richardson directed me to open my suitcase outside from that point forward upon returning from staying at my parents' house. The water bug incident was another thing that made me not want to go home again.

∞

At dinner on our first evening back together, Mrs. Richardson pulled out slides that could be viewed through a pair of binoculars. There were pictures of Weeki Wakki World where women dressed as mermaids danced and glided through the water in big aquariums. And Busch Gardens where pink flamingos lived by the hundreds. I decided right then and there I wanted to go to Florida one day.

∞

We finished the evening with my pleasure and delight. Mrs. Richardson played a beautiful song from a new piece of sheet music she brought home from vacation. It was from a Charles Dickens' play called *Oliver* about an orphan.

Where is love, does it fall from skies above? Is it underneath the willow tree that I've been dreaming of?

I loved the song and was happy to sing it standing there

by Mrs. Richardson while she sorted out the notes on her organ.

15

Mrs. Richardson liked me so much that she asked me to stay on at her house beyond the summer. She said that I could walk to my new school, the white school, from her house. So I stayed and I practice-walked to Star Elementary several times over the summer.

I took the windy black-topped road that ran past Mrs. Richardson's from the black section of Star toward downtown. I went past the Haskalo's ranch style brick house that sat on a rise diagonally from Mrs. Richardson's, then past the Russell's mansion with its duck pond out front, and on around a big curve past Dr. Scarborough's office which was across the street from the two-story Presbyterian church. I took the shortcut behind the church and climbed the incline to the railroad track that ran parallel to Highway 220. I followed the railroad a short distance south before taking a little path that landed me on the west side of the highway. My new school was on the other side of the road facing toward the west.

The main part of the school was a red-brick two-story building. There was a large white-columned entry that made the building look inviting. Out front of the school was a long crescent-shaped driveway where the school buses would load and unload students. The immense grounds contained tall bushy oak and elm trees that looked as old as the town. The trees cast shade all around the school. I couldn't wait until September when I would begin seventh grade and make a new best friend. Although I liked Mrs. Richardson and being at her house, I was lonely for someone my own age.

∞

Mrs. Richardson did not rise on my first day of school the way Mama always had with me and my brothers. I dressed and ate a bowl of Rice Krispies before setting off to Star Elementary. When I arrived, buses were lined in the driveway just as I pictured them. Kids and adults that I took to be the teachers, milled around on the sidewalk. One of the adults asked me what grade I was in.

"Seventh grade," I said with as much authority as I could bring forward given the butterflies in my stomach.

"Over there." The teacher pointed toward a cluster of students on the far edge of the crowd. I spotted Ola Mae, the only dark-skinned kid among a group of whites. Although Ola Mae had never been my close friend at Brutonville, I was glad to see a familiar face. The teacher standing with the group asked me my name.

"Levonne Gaddy," I told him.

He looked over the list and made a check. With an efficient manner, the man said, "Stand over here. We'll be going to the classroom in a few minutes."

I went straight for Ola Mae. "How you doing?" I talked to

her but my eyes scanned all the kids clustered together in small groups.

"Fine."

"You have a good summer?"

"Sure did."

I barely registered anything that Ola Mae said. She stood out from everyone because in addition to being brown, she was fat. All the white kids and I were much thinner than Ola Mae.

Ola Mae had been part of a less outgoing girls' group at Brutonville than my friends. As she chatted on, I thought about which girl might become my best friend at Star Elementary. There was a pair of twins with straight blond hair; there were several girls with bouncy brown hair flipped on the ends. There was one black-haired girl with wire braces on her teeth. Most of the kids seemed to take me and Ola Mae in as their eyes darted around the crowd.

The teacher, who I heard other kids call Mr. Welch, led us to a building that was old and made of similar red bricks as the main building. Inside the classroom the ceiling was high. The window frames were wood and painted white, not steel like at Brutonville. The light seemed dim, shady inside, cool in warm times, but toasty from the big cream-colored radiators in fall and winter. Mr. Welch organized us right away. He seated me beside Ola Mae.

∞

Mr. Welch was handsome enough with his dark straight hair and dark-rimmed glasses even with his facial skin potted from a former acne problem. He was a tall middle-aged

149

man who walked with shorter and quicker steps than most men. He was very serious.

"Alright class, I want you to welcome our new students this year. They have come from another school."

Mr. Welch proceeded to introduce me and Ola Mae. I did not want this attention. The air was thick with eleven- and twelve-year-old energy. Kids shuffled in their seats. I stood, but wanted to shrink into my seat. *Why couldn't we just pretend we were not new and just get on with it?* After saying our names out loud and having us stand up, Mr. Welch continued, "Alright class. When I call your name, come up and get your books."

The classroom was filled with clean kids. Two thirds of the class were girls and the other third was boys. It was odd to sit among kids that looked like me. My skin and eyes were light like theirs. I looked at Ola Mae. She filled her desk. She looked different—with slumping shoulders, head and eyes turned downward in a shy sort of way, unlike the white kids who sat head upright and were animated in their physical actions. Ola Mae seemed self-conscious when she walked to get her books. Even though she was heavy, she was quiet in her movements. Everyone watched her walk. I felt embarrassed.

∞

Mr. Welch said we would have recess before changing classes. I had not changed classes at Brutonville. This was going to be a new experience that I looked forward to. Later, we were going to the math teacher's class. As I rose from my seat, I smiled at several of the girls. They grouped and

150

talked in three or foursomes and filed out of the room. Ola
Mae and I were the only girls left. I looked at her and smiled.
I shrugged my shoulders and said, "Let's go." She smiled
and in a cumbersome way raised her body from her chair. I
waited for Ola Mae as she proceeded past the row of desks,
making soft-heavy–step-noises as she walked.

Outside, the boys raced around the playground and made
loud noises. The girls stood in circles and chattered. Ola
Mae and I began a conversation.

"So what do you think of Mr. Welch?" I inquired.

"He's okay."

"He's kinda cute."

Ola Mae smiled and said, "Yeah."

I was not used to having a conversation with her. She
seemed shy and also seemed as though she was entertained
by things that I did not see. She giggled a lot. I spent most
of my time watching the girls and trying to remember their
names.

"What's her name?" I asked tipping my head toward a
particular girl. Sometimes Ola Mae knew the name and
sometimes she didn't. "She seems nice," I would add about
a girl if she looked our way and smiled even slightly.

At one point a group of boys ran in our direction. I smiled
as Richard approached more closely. Ten feet from us, he
skidded, causing gravel to fly out from under his feet at
us. The boys from his group laughed, Ola Mae giggled, but
my smile evaporated. All during recess, not one student
spoke to me or Ola Mae. I wondered how I was going to go

about changing the situation. It occurred to me that making friends might not be as easy as I had imagined.

∞

Of all the girls in my seventh grade class at Star Elementary, Mary Poole saw it fit to begin a relationship with me. Mary seemed a bit shy, but she had a nice smile. She was both small and short for a twelve year old. She was stiff in her movements as if something impeded her head swiveling on her neck. You could tell she was poor because she wore white turned-down socks with lace-up brown-leather shoes, and had oily hair. I didn't care. I was ready to make some real friends. I was already tired of hanging out with Ola Mae as she had begun teasing me about my long "giraffe neck" and giggling. Mary Pool lived close enough to Mrs. Richardson's to walk to see me, so I invited her over.

∞

"This is a nice house." Mary's eyes took in Mrs. Richardson's screened-in front porch and her front yard bordered by flowering plants.

I asked, "What do you want to do?" as I walked Mary up the flank of stairs from the carport to the private entrance into my room.

"I don't care. Whatever you want to do." Mary was a very agreeable and easygoing girl.

I showed her my room, pointing out the twin bed where I slept beneath the big window and watched stars at night. Mary looked around the room at the drapes on the windows and at the carpet. I could tell she was impressed. I clicked on the radio and pulled out a teen magazine with Sajid Kahn, from *My Friend Maya*, and the Monkees on the cover and we began talking just as if we had been friends forever. I relaxed, believing that things were going to work out at Star Elementary School after all.

∞

For a week at the new school, I rode along on the excitement of my new friendship with Mary. During spelling in Mr. Welch's classroom, I smiled at Mary every chance I got. I also reflected on how Ola Mae stood alone on the sidewalk at recess. *She will just have to make her own friends* I thought *instead of chasing everybody away with her stink.* I had heard kids whisper that she needed to take a bath. It was true. She smelled of underarm odor some days.

Then at recess one day on my way to meet Mary, I was blocked by Carlene Rush. "I know you have been trying to make friends with Mary," she said. I thought *how nice to have another girl who wants to talk with me.* I gave her all of my attention. "Mary is my friend." Carlene and I stared at one another for a moment. "Levonne, it is time for you to go back to Ola Mae. You need to stick with your own kind and we'll stick with ours." Carlene's words stung like a bunch of bees and hit like a kick in the rump. I froze for a moment as Carlene walked away to Mary and engaged her in going outside.

I spent the rest of the day feeling the shame of being put in my place and was desperate for a new place. I daydreamed about the members of the Monkees singing group, of Sajid Kahn, and the beautiful Russell mansion through the woods beyond Mrs. Richardson's house, where I would have loved to live. When reality injected itself into my daydreams, it came in the form of Carlene's words reverberating through my mind—"stick with your own kind." I looked at Ola Mae and began to resent her more than ever. *Who made her my kind?* I wondered.

16

The "new math" that Mrs. McAlister taught made no sense to me. I was certain she was putting Ola Mae and me down during her class. Who can pay attention to new math taught by a person who thought of you as a "niggra?" It was 1966. We weren't even Negros anymore. We were black.

Mrs. McAlister was pretty enough. She had brown hair that she wore in a puffy style that complimented her dark rimmed glasses. She was the seventh and eighth grade math and social studies teacher. I wished she was more like Teresa's mother, Mrs. Johnson, my fourth grade teacher. Being best friends with Teresa and visiting Mrs. Johnson's house had made me feel important, smart and popular.

Barbara was Mrs. McAlister's girl. She was at my grade level, the same as Teresa had been. Teresa was black. Barbara was white. Barbara examined me from a distance with her eyes. Mrs. McAlister did the same kind of examining. It was nothing like the tactile affection expressed for me by Teresa and Mrs. Johnson. No expressions coming from Barbara's lips, such as, "your hair is soft." No smiles and arm squeezes from Mrs. McAlister.

During her lesson about the South's agricultural past,

Mrs. McAlister spoke of blacks as "niggras" over and over again. Not "Negros" as everyone with respect might call some of the people from whom I emerged; but "niggra," which sounded too close to the worst word that a white could say to or about a black.

With each "niggra" Mrs. McAlister chirped out, I cringed in my seat. I felt my head slump and I sank lower into my torso. I wanted to disappear. Mrs. McAlister did not pass out any of the acknowledgements that I was accustomed to from teachers during my years at Brutonville. No "Levonne is a natural leader," or "You're a very smart young lady," or "We'd be delighted for you to come spend the weekend with our daughter at our house." Instead there were those distant disrobing eyes of Barbara's and her mother's. They maintained the constant distance where never, not even accidentally, do you dare touch "one of them."

To top it all off, Mrs. McAlister gave me my first F. I failed new math. It was like a foreign language that I had never heard before. At first I thought it must be a mistake but later, I thought *maybe I am ignorant, dumber than the whites.* Even though I looked like them with my fair skin, my wavy hair and green eyes, having black blood in me might make me stupid, less brainy than even the worst behaved white boy.

∞

Ola Mae and I were seated side by side in all the classrooms. Our last names both began with a "G." Everyone assumed that she and I were best friends because we came to Star Elementary together from Brutonville. But this false belief did not matter to the white teachers or the white students. Ola Mae and I were forced to be friends or to have no one. So we spent recess standing together on the sidewalk while the other kids roamed around the grounds of the school. Ola Mae and I shared information about the people we had in common from our neighborhood or antagonized each other about anything we could find to pick on each other about.

"Your neck looks like a giraffe's neck," Ola Mae chuckled as she hurled the comment.

"That damn dress looks like it's getting a little too small for you." I found a new power and pleasure in using cuss words. Ola Mae always reacted.

"What would your mama say if she heard you talk like that?"

"Who the hell cares?" In those moments I didn't care, although I would never have used the same language in front of any adult.

"Girl, God is gonna punish you for talking like that."

"I don't give a fuck." The "F" word was the worst and made Ola Mae cringe the most.

To add flavor to our recess, a group of boys led by Richard gave us nicknames. "Hey Bozo and Snowflake. What ya up to?" Richard and his boys called us these names throughout the year at recess and during lunch. Their words brought snickers from anyone close enough to hear.

Ola Mae and I accepted our names without a fight. We even smiled sometimes. I guess I was Snowflake because of my fair-skinned complexion, but I could have been Bozo, because for the first time in my life, I began acting like a class clown. I made exaggerated comical faces in reaction to things around me. Sometimes I brought my body into the act and added to the effect of my facial contortion. It made kids laugh, though they still did not make an effort to make me their friend.

The weird thing was that even though Richard made fun of us with his name calling, I liked him. After all, he talked to us, even though his words were abusive. Some attention was better than none at all.

∞

At the end of it all, I judged my first year of involvement in the southern experiment called integration a big flop. Mrs. McAlister and her "niggras" and Richard with the Snowflake and Bozo names, the absence of my old friends and no real new ones, the forced friendship with Ola Mae and the "F" in new math fast added up to my worst school year ever. Seventh grade at Star Elementary was the pits.

17

Summer break of 1967 was welcomed. I could not stand myself by the end of seventh grade. While I slipped naturally enough into the class clown role, I felt lessened by it. I respected myself less for disrupting class with my buffoonery, regardless as to how funny I might have thought I was with my exaggerated facial expressions. I had become just a memory of the respected girl leader that I was at Brutonville, and I had felt powerless to change things.

Anyone could have seen if they cared to look, that failing Mrs. McAllister's new math bothered me. The report card's stock weight manilla paper was rippled by eraser abrasion beneath the "F" that, finally, I had surrendered to and inked back in by my own hand. I had never failed a subject. Neither Mrs. Richardson, the teachers, nor my parents commented on the obvious defacement of the card.

I felt less-than the white kids. They sealed off their circles of friendship from me, aside from Mary for a brief few weeks. And never once did anyone speak specifically and directly about the "new integration" in which Ola Mae, I and the white kids in my class participated. We were not given a guidebook of rules for behavior and we needed guidance desperately. We were all, black kids and white, left to figure out integration and make it what it was going to be on our own.

So the end of the school year was extra special. No more kids making fun of me, calling me Snow Flake or rejecting me by telling me to stick with my own kind. No more failing subjects. No more humiliation from clowning around. I had survived the school year and at least I had Mrs. Richardson in my life. I had escaped the liquor-infested weekends at my parents' house for a year by the time summer break arrived.

I convinced myself that I was a grandchild to her and was ever alert for the day that she was to say to me, "Levonne, just call me Grandmama." Of course that day never came but, my naiveté and optimism shielded me from the hurt I might have felt had I been wiser.

The absence of cash payment for what I did for Mrs. Richardson, in part made me think we might be more family than employer/employee. Since I liked to work, I didn't mind my chores. Dish washing, vacuuming, dusting and cleaning the bathroom, putting dirty clothes in the washing machine then hanging them out to dry or putting them in the dryer, ironing the laundered linens, mowing the lawn and pulling weeds from the flower garden did not seem like too much work. I was glad not to be sleeping in the room with my older and two younger brothers or witnessing the fallout from my parents' boozing.

At the beginning of the summer, Mrs. Richardson asked, "Would you like to baby-sit the little girl across the street?"

I would earn twenty dollars a week for six weeks. One hundred twenty dollars seemed like a fortune to me.

"Yes ma'am. I would like to babysit her."

Being with five-year-old Tina Haskalo was a breeze. While her parents worked their management jobs at Star's hosiery mill, Tina and I spent the summer days together. At age twelve, my workday started before Mrs. Haskalo left for work and ended when she arrived home again.

Even though Tina was Jewish (something I knew nothing about), a middle class white kid's life is what the experience schooled me about. I enjoyed every minute of the lessons. Tina was the same age as my hyperactive brother, Frankie. At nearly six years of age, she didn't know anything about racism. She looked up to me.

I had missed enough of my own childhood to find the activities that Tina and I engaged in for six weeks to be just what I needed. Along with checkers and monopoly, Tina had a piano and a record player with a few good records including a favorite "Up on the Roof."

"Let's play it again, Tina," I said from my place on Tina's bedroom floor.

"Okay," Tina responded from her position hovering over a coloring book. She lifted the record player's speckled grey arm and replaced it at the beginning of the 45 rpm record.

When this old world starts getting me down
And people are just too much for me to face
I climb way up to the top of the stairs
And all my cares just drift right into space.

Tina had makeup that her sister in college had given her.

She had giant hair rollers that she used to set her down-to-the-middle-of-her-back thick brown hair. After thirty minutes of dragging around the portable hair dryer with the vented plastic cap, we unrolled her hair and rejoiced at the resulting bouncy curls before playing chopsticks on the piano. Tina's family kept a large tin of Charles' potato chips in the house. For the first time in my life, I ate all the chips I wanted.

In addition to the great play things and the chips, Tina was a great kid. Even though she was the same age as Frankie, her calmness was tenfold over his. She acted as old as me. It must have come from her being in a family with only adults–her parents and a grown brother and sister.

∞

Weekdays with Tina were great, but weekends became a different matter that summer. Boredom reared its head. The novelty of living with a seventy-something-year-old white woman with money was wearing off. I wanted friends my age.

When Mrs. Richardson's, five- and four-year-old grandkids visited, I was excited. One Sunday morning, I was allowed to go along to Mrs. Richardson's church to look after Kathy and Rick. I had not visited a white person's church before.

The rituals of following a schedule of ordered standing and sitting and of singing from hymnals fascinated me. But Mrs. Richardson told me afterward that I was too noisy with telling her grandkids to be quiet. She said that they weren't the misbehaviors, but it was I that misbehaved with my nattering at them. I guess I was nervous with all the schedule-following. It was not like the black folks' Green Grove United Church of God's spontaneous, spirit-move-your-actions that I was accustomed to. She never took me to her church again.

On the Sundays that followed, when Mrs. Richardson went to church, I went into her bedroom, which was filled with Estee Lauder perfume and Aquanet hairspray smells. On her television I watched my favorite shows and tried to figure out, from The Rev. Billy Graham's guidance, how I could repent for my sins.

After lessons on repenting, although Mrs. Richardson told me never to touch her electric organ, I couldn't resist. It was the most fun thing to do when she was out. I tried to play some of the songs that she had me sing in the evenings to her playing. I managed to escape her wrath by returning the tone buttons and knobs back the way she had left them. If I changed something, because I just had to hear what a note sounded like in a different tone, I set it back as she had left it. She did not have to tell me to keep my hands off her organ again, because she didn't detect my fiddling with it.

I figured out that if you match your fingers on the keys with where the notes were in relation to the lines and spaces of the sheet music, you could make a tune that sounded kind of like the song. I learned to play on one hand the notes from the song in the Charles Dickens play of the same name "Oliver." That was my favorite song that Mrs. Richardson played. Over and over I played tune that went with the words:

Where is love?
Does it fall from skies above?
Is it underneath the willow tree?
That I've been dreaming of?

Mrs. Richardson did not allow me to spend the money I made from my baby-sitting job. She opened an account in my name at Wachovia Bank in downtown Star and my checks were deposited there. Two weeks before school started, Mrs. Richardson took me to Belk's Department Store in Asheboro where my Great Aunt Annie worked, and we used my money to buy new dresses for school. Mrs. Richardson was impressed with Aunt Annie's peronality.

"Your aunt is well-spoken," she told me at the start of the twenty-five-minute drive down Highway 220 back to Star. She proposed that instead of me going home to my parents' house when she went off to Richmond, Virginia to visit her millionaire daughter, that I might like to stay with Aunt Annie. I said that would be dandy. I had always liked my Aunt Annie, though I had not stayed at her house since I was one year old.

18

Though I would have liked to have gone with Mrs. Richardson to visit her millionaire daughter in Richmond, Virginia, I was also pleased to be with my aunt. Aunt Annie's house sat in a rural part of the town, just outside the small city of Asheboro.

Her house was where my mother and father met and where my family lived for a brief period during my father's hospitalization when I was one year old. The house was an older, weathered-wood, two-story on a weedy plot of several acres. It was a former farm house, surrounded by a few dilapidated structures. The house had a large screened-in back porch and an unscreened front porch. On the first floor were an ample kitchen and a dining room with table and chairs that matched. Off the dining room was Aunt Annie's room. There was a fireplace in her bedroom that she used for heating in the winter. Also on the bottom floor was a living room with a sofa in front of a large picture window that looked out onto the road leading to and away from the house.

Aunt Annie had indoor plumbing which meant a bathroom on both floors. Three bedrooms filled the upstairs.

One large bedroom contained three double beds and was used for company. Another bedroom with bunk beds was where my distant twin cousins Daniel and Fred slept. They were visiting Aunt Annie also. They were older than me. Both seniors. Fred was a star football player at the white high school that he and Daniel attended.

Aunt Annie's house was filled with treasures. Her glass front cupboards were filled with colorful crystal and dishes. The sofa in the upstairs hallway was draped with clothing from the department store where Aunt Annie worked. Visitors to the house were expected to go through the clothing to see if what was there might fit. If it did, we were allowed to take it. My favorite dress from the pile was a purple dress with white dots and a large white collar. It was a little too long but a quick hemming and pressing job took care of that.

Once Aunt Annie knew your size, she would bring things home from the store for you, sometimes still on the hanger. The house was a grand contrast to the skimpy and grit-covered house of my mother's and the ordered, sanitary surroundings of Mrs. Richardson's. Aunt Annie had lots of stuff but there was also chaos, which made it more challenging and fun to find things.

∞

At twelve, flirtatious play with older boys was delightful. I loved to yank on Daniel's shirt or stomp on his toes and run away from him urging, "I bet you can't catch me." Daniel took my flirting in stride, neither drawn to me because of it nor repulsed by it.

I was not as interested in Fred, though he was more handsome with a little mustache and a strong build; he was just not the same kind of fun as his brother. I loved when Daniel chased me and loved it more when he caught me and tickled me. I felt safe. I had wrestled with my brothers my entire life.

Fred was a popular boy at his integrated high school. He was engaged in the act of breaking the interracial relationship taboo by having a white girlfriend. Melissa was her name. Her family didn't know about them. She was sure her dad would go ballistic if he did, but those of us in my cousin Fred's family were accepting of their relationship.

One afternoon near the end of my stay with Aunt Annie, she ran a quick errand. I felt fine about staying behind with Fred. I stood in Aunt Annie's living room and watched through the picture window as she drove away from the house in her wooden-side-paneled station wagon.

Before she was out of sight, Fred was by my side, pushing me toward and onto the sofa. On top of me, Fred pecked at my face with his lips. I struggled. While my mouth was open, asking Fred what he was doing, he placed his mouth over mine and shoved his tongue in. His spit was bitter. A nasty, slimy taste. I gagged. I wanted to spit the foreign fluid from my mouth, and while distracted by the filthy taste, Fred yanked my shorts and underpants off with one swift jerk and with less effort than I would have ever imagined possible.

Fred was back on me before I could sit up straight and get my balance. I pushed at him and at the same time felt embarrassed by my rejection of him. I somehow believed that it was wrong for me not to like Fred, to be mean to him in any way. I was paralyzed by the feelings of embarrassment and shame over my own meanness for telling him to stop and about my nakedness. With Fred on top of me pressing the fronts of his shoulders into my body, I became motionless. And from one of the motionless moments, I disappeared to some place outside of myself.

∞

I felt air filling my lungs as Fred lifted himself off me and scrambled out of the room. I grabbed my clothes from the floor, and in my aunt's bathroom, clutching my shorts and underwear to my chest, I touched where it burned, then looked at blood streaks on my hand. It hurt as if salt had been poured on an open cut. I nursed my dazed self there with one of my aunt's beautiful guest washcloths. I washed between my legs and trembled. I wondered what on earth had happened. Quick, strong Fred had come and gone in an instant. I could never have anticipated what was to happen before it happened. There had been no warning. I had had no concern. I had been a happy girl, innocent and comfortable between my legs. My shame for having caused what happened was a message to me that I should never speak of it to anyone. The rest of my time at Aunt Annie's was an uncomfortable blur.

∞

It was late summer Sunday noon and I was back at Mrs. Richardson's. With my recent trip to Aunt Annie's and Fred still in my mind, I decided to ride my blue bicycle to my parents' house.

I steered off the edge of the road's pavement onto grass and rocks. The vibration from the lumps of Bermuda grass and quartz rock made me vibrate all over. Back onto the pavement, I stood on my bicycle and pedaled as hard as I could. The warm air forced my hair back then thrashed it about my face. Down the incline I went, daring myself to go faster. From a seated position, after making the turn into Dunn-Green town, I huffed hard and pedaled the rest of the way to my parents' house.

Standing in the front yard under the shade of a jacaranda tree were three neighbor boys and my brothers, Lee and Dale. They were animated as they talked over one another. They spoke of their trip to the carnival that was making its way through North Carolina counties. It had opened in Biscoe the day before.

"Man did you see those titties jiggle 'round?" said Bobo, who was a year younger than me. All the boys laughed. I sucked in my breath and stood still with my bicycle leaning against the inside of my leg. I could not believe what they were saying with me listening. I had seen a hoochie coochie show stage once. A half-dressed woman made exaggerated hip gyrations and exposed a great deal of breast. Men, women, children, blacks and whites stood around the stage with either wide, shocked expressions or smiles while a man with a microphone bid people to come on in and get a better look.

Another boy said, "Lee, Lee, tell us 'bout that one that took that coke bottle and stuck it all the way up her thing." I pushed off on my bicycle away from the laughter, thinking about how much I hated all those filthy boys. But what was left in my mind was the picture of a naked woman, gyrating around a stage, presenting to the crowd of salivating men, boys and women a cola bottle, in the manner a magician might present a rabbit for his audience's examination after pulling it out of a top hat.

At the front door steps of my parents' house, I imagined the hoochie coochie woman with her back toward the crowd, her feet spread wide apart, leaned forward with the bottle positioned near her opening, primed to shove it up her cavity.

"She sucked that thing up in her without even using her hands," Lee reported.

"Naw she didn't," Bobo said over the boys howling with laughter.

"Then she shot it back out and caught it with one hand." Lee was fourteen, the oldest of all the boys. His last words caused the boys to disperse, all looking satiated by the graphic descriptions. I felt sad and mad that the boys, and my brothers, were focused on the sex organs of a woman. *How far might they take their interest in a female's body?* I wondered.

∞

The front door stood open. My father's truck was gone from the yard, so I did not expect him to be inside. I did expect my mother to be there. I pushed down the kick stand of my bicycle. The sand on the concrete front steps crunched beneath my rubber soled sneakers as I stepped. In the living room of my parents' house, I smelled the usual cigarette smoke, sweaty shoes and the acidic pungency of the cockroach pee wafting in from beneath the house. "Hey Frankie," I greeted my five-and-a-half-year-old brother as he rose from his position on the floor in front of the bookcase where he had been looking at an encyclopedia. He hugged me around my waist.

Frankie's hair was tightly curled from not being combed yet that day. His face had streaks of dirt on it that reminded me of children in the *National Geographic* books from lands high in the Andes Mountains. His hands were grubby as though they had not been washed all week. He was shirtless and his feet were bare and covered with dust accented by the dry marks formed from water drips.

"What you doing home?" Frankie smiled with such intensity that it appeared he might burst into laughter. He was always such a happy kid.

"Came to see you. Where's Mama." Being nowhere in sight, I listened for signs of her in the bedroom or kitchen, both of which were not in my direct view.

"In there," Frankie pointed to the open door of my parents' bedroom before returning back to the floor and one of the encyclopedias from an old set that my father had brought home from the Allens' house. Bound with a deep red cover and emboldened with gold letters, Frankie took the book into his lap and began gazing at a picture of a Gila monster.

I walked through the living room, feeling slight grittiness beneath my feet from much tracking in and out of the room by my three brothers, father and mother. The tall book case that I tried to keep straightened when I lived with my parents was disheveled. I brushed my hand along the shelf, then wiped the dust from my hand onto my shorts.

Mama lay on her side facing the middle of the bed. Standing over her, I called, "Mama. Mama. Wake up." My mother did not move. I did not know whether the smell of alcohol that filled my nostrils was from that day or from my memory. But with each of my mother's exhales, the odor seemed to grow stronger. "Mama," I leaned over her and called louder. I felt the warmth of my mother's skin in my hand as I raised her right arm, felt the weight of it for a few moments, and then dropped it. The arm landed on her side with the dull sound of body part against body before the hand slid, palm open, onto the aged sheet that covered the mattress. Mama was knocked out. My needs would have to wait.

Back in the living room, I stood and watched Frankie for a few minutes. He was amazing. He couldn't read that much and he was still so interested in those encyclopedias. I looked at his dirty body and his uncombed hair. I decided I would give him a bath. I walked past him to the kitchen. A half pail was left of the three buckets that held the water for my family.

The aluminum pan that my family used for washing sat beneath the kitchen table. I filled the pan with water and placed it on the electric stove element and turned the knob to the medium heat position.

While the water heated, I found my mother's hand mirror and took it with me to the outside toilet behind the house. I passed the garden with weed infested squash and cucumber plants and wondered how the hoochie coochie women came to work in a traveling carnival. How curious it all seemed to me.

I pushed the ripped burlap sack that served as the toilet's door aside and entered. Feces and urine smells filled my nose. I began to breathe shallowly.

In the privacy of the outdoor toilet, I straddled above a hole and with the mirror examined my private parts. I thought of the incident with Fred earlier in the week. Since the day at Aunt Annie's when I found myself in her bathroom wondering how to stop the burning, I had become interested in the sight of myself. So whenever I had privacy, one of the first things I did was look and wonder about the whole business of sexual organs. *What is hymen? How do you get a baby out of such a small opening? Am I still a virgin?*

∞

I positioned my blue bicycle on the carport before climbing the wooden stairs to the back of Mrs. Richardson's house and to my room. She had gone out to visit her friend in Seagrove for the afternoon. The outside door to my room had been left unlocked since Mrs. Richardson decided that she did not want me to have a key of my own into the whole house anymore. She thought that leaving the door unlocked to my room from the outside, then locking the kitchen door that joined my room to the rest of the house so nobody could enter her house when she was gone was a good idea.

I liked my room a lot. That was not the question for me. I did not like being locked out of the rest of the house.

I sat down on the bench in front of the dressing table in

my room. I looked at the mirror laying there with the pink plastic handle. Mrs. Richardson's daughter, Macy, from Troy had given me a pink mirror, brush and comb set the Christmas before. I looked at the mirror and I looked at myself in the mirror. Sweat beaded around the edges of my hair. Brown curls lay flat, pasted against my skin. I rubbed my finger over the sweat. I rubbed the sweat beads off my nose. I frowned at myself in the mirror.

The boys' words about the hoochie coochie woman crowded into my head. I rose somewhat like a robot, holding the mirror in my hand and walked to the locked door between my room and the kitchen. I peered through the window panes that were the top half of the door. I could almost smell the pound cake that I knew was beneath the cake cover on the kitchen table. I jiggled the door knob.

I counted two window panes in the top portion of the door. The windows were separated by a wooden panel and held in place by strips of molding. The door and moldings were painted a powdery pale green. I touched the molding trim. I rubbed my hands along its edges. It was rough. The paint had tiny bumps in it. I drove a fingernail between the molding and the wood panel. I had watched my father remove and replace windows before in many of the houses where we had lived. I began to look around my room for an instrument that might help me do a similar type of job as he had done with windows in his life. Not finding anything flat and hard and long in my room, I went downstairs to the basement and found an old butter knife in a tray of tools. I took the knife and a small hammer back to the bedroom.

Without a clue at that time about the reasons for the anxiety-ridden compulsion to explore an adult's things when they left me alone, I removed piece by piece, the molding from around one window. After removing the pane, I reached my hand through the opening to unlock the door from the other side. A click of the lock and the door was open. I then replaced the window, as I did not want Mrs. Richardson to return home and find her window pane out. Then I began to ramble through anything of hers that might help me form questions and uncover answers to the mystery of her and of me together.

19

The kids at Star Elementary were the same kids in eighth grade as had been in seventh grade. Their attitude must have been the same also—stick with your own kind—because still nobody made an effort to become a friend. It continued to be just me and Ola Mae.

Richard and his friends, the same boys that called Ola Mae and me Snowflake and Bozo, instituted a new game that began early in the year and continued throughout the rest of the school year.

From the cafeteria after lunch, my eighth grade class began its way back to our classroom in line formation. But once outside and with the two teachers, Mrs. McAlister and Mr. Ray lagging behind and out of sight, all thirty plus class-mates began trotting and running. I trotted too. Ola Mae, because of her weight, did not run.

Once in the classroom, with Ola Mae behind everyone else and the teachers further behind still, we ran to our seats and sat down. When Ola Mae reached the room, out of breath, she lumbered through the door and Richard shouted, "Pick up your feet." Like a robot, I along with every other student, smart or dumb, lifted our feet off the floor and held them in the air until Ola Mae took her seat.

For thirty awkward seconds, Ola Mae wobbled across the front of the class to her seat with everyone watching, including me. Once she sat down, all the feet dropped to the floor with loud thumps and thuds. A burst of laughter and giggles followed.

A minute later, Mr. Ray entered the classroom to complete silence. Innocence and obedience took over the classroom with his presence, and I acted toward Ola Mae as if the whole thing did not happen day after day. We did not speak about the feet raising incidents during break when I stood with Ola Mae and expressed myself with multi-word cursing combinations— "Mother fucker. Son of a bitch. God Dammit to hell."

∞

I was sick of Ola Mae's underarm odor, of the boys calling me Snowflake and of Mrs. McAlister's 'niggra this, niggra that' comments that followed us on into her eighth grade social studies class. I dreamed of reuniting with my former friends from Brutonville, though I remembered that my best friend Teresa would not be among them. Graduation from Star Elementary School to East Montgomery High School could not come too fast for me.

20

"Don't let the flag touch the ground Levonne." Mrs. Richardson was particular about the American flag that she displayed every day in honor of her grandson, Hal, who was flying a helicopter in Vietnam. I was very careful to keep it away from the ground and to bring it in at the start of rain.

On the summer June Saturday morning of 1968, as soon as I hung the flag in the brace mounted by Mrs. Richardson's front door, my attention shifted to mowing the front yard. It was one of my favorite things to do. I poured gas into the lawnmower tank, while the smell of fuel stung the insides of my nose and made me sneeze.

The rope on the engine was stiff, but I had developed a way of yanking it just right to make the machine fire and ready itself for being pushed and pulled across the yard. The sun was bright overhead. It felt good on my arms and legs. I liked getting tanned in the summer. I liked the way it gave me a golden glow even if it made my freckles pop out a bit more.

Starting at the driveway I pushed the mower to the edge of Mrs. Richardson's property where it joined the next door neighbors, Judy and Ken's yard. I took pride in making straight even-spaced tracks in the grass. The rhythm of going back and forth across the yard, the hum of the mower and the smell of cut grass seduced me into wakeful dreaming about high school.

I felt a little sad when I remembered that Teresa would not be at East Montgomery, but other friends from Brutonville would. Beverly, Avis, and Deborah. I looked forward to seeing them. I couldn't wait to talk with them about their lives and share my life with them. I wondered how impressed they might be by my living with Mrs. Richardson. After all, none of them had a chance to live with somebody who had a millionaire daughter and served tea in china cups at a canasta party. I wondered how many of them knew how to set a table with silver and china, crystal and cloth napkins.

In the midst of imagining going on a double date with one of my friends, a louder roar drowned the roar of the lawn mower. I looked toward the road that went past Mrs. Richardson's, for several miles from downtown Star to the Dunn-Green Town turnoff, to see large camouflage colored army trucks lumbering down the road. I pushed the choke lever downward and shut off the motor. One, two, three trucks passed. Two jeeps. Then more trucks. I stood with my hands on my hips when not waving at the soldiers. The large tires, the greens and tans, the metal, the roar of engines and the sound of tires rolling on the asphalt hypnotized me.

Some of the soldiers were white, some were black. Some of them stood on the backs of trucks and waved. I stopped counting after reaching five. A knot of excitement formed in the center of my stomach and radiated toward my throat.

If I had been a little younger than my almost fourteen years, I would have jumped up and down and laughed out loud. I would have run behind the last truck and yelled words like "Come back. Talk with me." But I was older, so I stood still and waved, laughter giggle being the only sound anyone might have heard. I wondered where the soldiers were going. I suppressed an impulse to jump on my bicycle and follow them. With half a yard yet to mow, I finished the job in a quarter of the time that it had taken me to do the first part of the yard and told Mrs. Richardson that I was going to ride down to my parents' house for a visit.

∞

Mama was hanging clothes on the line when I emerged on my bicycle from the path through the woods into my family's side yard.

"Whatcha doing home?" Mama smiled with the matter-of-factness about her that I liked.

"Visiting." I stood beside my mother, straddling the bicycle and watched her hang my brothers' shirts one by one, joining each at a shoulder by a wooden clothes pin.

"What's Mrs. Richardson up to today?"

"Resting."

Mama took a few more shirts from the clothes basket. "Gloria and them are preparing for a big cookout."

"Yeah?"

"They're waiting for Francis and her family to come down from Charlotte."

"Well, I saw a big bunch of soldiers coming down this way this morning."

"Really? I haven't seen any, but I heard they were going to be doing maneuvers in the woods around here." She tipped her head toward the trees from which I had emerged a moment earlier.

As I positioned myself to ride again, I reflected on how good it felt to see and talk with my mother there at the clothesline. I filled my lungs with the fragrances of fresh air, laundry soap and the mildest scent of Clorox. In the midst of feeling good with my mother and enjoying the smell of the laundry, I cringed at my father's voice that suddenly boomed from inside the house.

"Goddammit. I told her to cook the fish before it spoiled." I looked at my mother. Her face tensed. At the same moment as my father was roaring on about the fish, my four-teen-year-old brother Lee emerged from the house and pro-ceeded to where Mama and I were standing by the clothes-line. Lee was the handsomest boy in Star. His curly hair, brown eyes and creamy tanned skin were beautiful. I admired how smart he was too.

"You gonna have to leave him, Mama. He can't keep treat-ing you like he's treating you."

"Aw now stop talking that way about your father."

"You can't keep puttin' up with it."

I had not heard Lee talk about this to our mother before. And as much as the idea of Mama leaving the family dis-turbed me, I could see where Lee was coming from. I full knew that the next step after Daddy roared around with his voice was to become physically violent. I added, "It's true Mama."

182

She took a cigarette from the pack resting atop the chopping block and lit it. She stood with the cigarette between her fore and middle finger and picked tobacco from the tip of her tongue with her thumb and fourth finger. Lee added, "If he hits you again, you need to leave and go up to Aunt Annie's and stay."

Mama looked out at the road. "We'll see. We'll see." She went back to hanging clothes on the line after placing her lit cigarette on the edge of the block.

∞

With Frankie on my handle bars, I rode down the path past Gloria's cousin's house to her front porch. "How you, Miss Levonne?" Gloria's grandmother, Ms. Lily, fanned herself with one of the Philips Funeral Home fans that every house in the black section of Star had in their living rooms in the summer. She spoke from an armchair. "What you doing down here in our neck of the woods?" Arm in arm, Frankie and I climbed the step onto the porch.

"Just came to visit."

"We miss you Honey. It's good to see you. And nice to see you too, Mr. Frankie." Ms. Lily started humming a church song beneath her breath. "Glory's back there in the back Child. Go on in. You'll find her."

I thanked Ms. Lily, then walked through the living room where Mr. Will, Gloria's grandfather, sat in a chair watching a TV commercial of the Lay's potato chip guy tempting, "I bet you can't eat just one," on their new color television.

In the kitchen, Frankie and I stopped to see Bernice, Gloria's aunt, making potato salad. Her bangs were wrapped around three pink sponge hair rollers. "Hey Sweetie. How you two?" She took another hot potato out of a large pot and began removing the skin before adding, "You sure are looking pretty." I touched my hair which was pulled back into a pony tail. During the summer it sparkled from the bleaching of the sun. I wiped at the moisture on my face formed from exertion and the humid air. I knew that I had turned a pleasant clover-honey shade from the sunshine. "Gloria's on the back porch." Frankie led the way. Gloria was putting a large bowl into a refrigerator already crowded with bottles of pop, a long pan of chicken and ribs in sauce and two pans of banana pudding. My mouth watered.

"Looks like y'all planning for a good time."

"You got that right. How you doing, Girl?" Gloria smiled. She was one year younger and a grade behind me in school. When I lived at my parents' house, she was the girl that I spent the most time with. Before Gloria and I could engage in significant conversation, we heard a car horn honk outside. Frankie zipped out of the back screened door. It slammed twice before Gloria caught it and pushed it open. She peered outside then yelled toward the interior of the house, "They're here."

Ms. Lily, Bernice and Gloria's mother, Chug, streamed down the back porch stairs one at a time and greeted Gloria's relatives from the city. Everyone laughed and said things like, "Look at that nice car" and "Glad y'all here 'cause we was getting mighty hungry." And there was "Oh so glad to see you" and hugging. Gloria's patch of backyard was surrounded by the dirt road that had brought the travelers to the house, the old horse barn, the well, and Gloria's grayed-wood home. The yard began swelling with people as other relatives joined in from the neighboring houses. Frankie raced around the back yard circling the crowd of people.

Gloria's aunt from Charlotte wore a pink dress that was tight fitting all over. The back was open in the shape of a triangle between her shoulders. Her hair was swirled at the back of her head in the shape of a soft-serve ice cream cone. Gloria's cousins, a girl who seemed to be about sixteen and a young man who might have been eighteen, disembarked last from the car.

Milton was Gloria's cousin. He wore a small, dark pair of shades. His hair was cut short. He was dressed in a white shirt with a black necktie. He said "As-salaam Alaikum" to Chug and Bernice.

Bernice said, "I'll assie lakum you. Take them shades off and come over here so I can see your face, Boy." Milton took off his shades and walked the few steps to Bernice. "Give your auntie a big hug." Bernice reached out and grabbed Milton. He grinned and as soon as the hug was over, put his shades back on.

After the family members greeted one another, Milton passed by me and said, "As-Salaam Alaikum, Little Sister." He tipped his head. I giggled. "That's the greeting from your Black Muslim brothers and sisters. It means *peace be with you.*"

I said, "Thank you and peace be with you too then."

"Your response would be Wa-Alaikum Salaam."

I repeated the words along with another giggle. "Wa-Alaikum Salaam." Gloria's cousin really stood out.

∞

People cooked on a grill that sat atop a round barrel with hot coals. The others arriving from the surrounding houses in Dunn-Green Town placed food on the long picnic tables that had been set up for the day's occasion.

Gloria and I talked on the back door steps as people sat at tables or milled around the back yard. All the activity was uncommon in my life with Mrs. Richardson. I suddenly realized that I missed the people of Dunn-Green Town in a way that I had not known until that moment. I felt warmth for everyone gathered around, laughing and talking over one another. In the midst of reflecting on the satisfaction of the experience and half listening to Gloria, I craned my neck to see what others were already giving their attention—an army jeep with four soldiers pulling into the backyard. The two soldiers in the front seat looked older than the two in the back.

"How you folks doing?" The soldier sitting beside the driver was closest to the crowd of people in the yard. He continued, "We're just out for a weekend drive. Mind if we stop for a while?"

Bernice whipped back real sassy-like, "Sure, don't mind. Y'all come on in." She motioned toward the picnic table.

The four soldiers climbed out of the jeep. My heart raced and I moved closer. They were all dressed in army green uniforms that had name patches sewn above their left shirt pockets. They wore shiny black boots that laced to the lower part of their calves. One dark-complexioned older soldier was tall and thin. The other older soldier, also black, was stocky. The two younger soldiers were both both shorter than the older soldiers, one light complexioned and the other closer in skin tone to the older men. The light skinned younger soldier looked at me and smiled. My stomach took a few flips.

The tall soldier reached out his hand to the first person he came to and said, "Hello. People call me Grease." He looked to be the age of Bernice and Chug–in his forties.

"Have something to drink," Bernice pointed at the cooler with ice and beer in it. At that invitation, the other older soldier, who said his name was Jerry, went back to the jeep and pulled out a case of beer that he took to the cooler and proceeded to fill to overflowing.

Lee, who was not big on hanging out at parties and who usually preferred staying at home to either watch sports on television or read a paperback novel, appeared. Mama was a few minutes behind him, carrying a package of hotdogs and some hot dog buns. I watched from the steps as Lee and the other boys examined the jeep.

Chug yelled, "There's plenty of food. Y'all dig in." I rose from my place on the door steps although something about the sight of the soldiers had diminished my appetite.

The young soldier, who didn't look one day older than my fifteen-year-old brother but had to be older because he was already in the army, introduced himself. "Hello." He shook hands with several people. "I'm Reuben Martinez." He had a slight build and the clothes he wore looked roomy on him.

He had fine features with dark eyebrows. "I like his name," I said to Gloria as Milton approached us.

"Alcohol is bad for black folks. It's the white man's way of killing us off." Gloria and I were caught off guard at her cousin's bold words. "The white man used a gun on the ones that had to be killed fast." Gloria and I exchanged glances. "Malcolm. Medgar. Martin." Milton looked at us when he said the names. He became more excited in his speech. "But the rest. They are going to die slowly from alcohol and drugs." Gloria and I sat and listened. Milton raised his hand to jab his forefinger into the air. "And every white man that thinks that blacks deserve the same dignity as they have is going to get mowed down just like Robert Kennedy this week and his brother five years ago."

I didn't know how to think about what Milton was saying. I had not thought that someone was out to get all the black people with alcohol, but it was true that a white man had killed Dr. Martin Luther King. I glanced at Reuben Martinez. He was sat at the same table as his army buddies, but did not eat.

"Those soldiers are fools. They are fighting the white man's war over in Vietnam when most of their parents didn't even have the right to vote when the war started." *Right to vote? What was Milton talking about* I wondered. "The Voting Rights Act gave black folks the right to vote whether they own property or not. No more literacy tests."

I asked, "What's a literacy test?"

"A test to determine whether someone can read. If you couldn't read, you couldn't vote." I thought about what Milton said. *Daddy couldn't read. Did that mean he couldn't vote until this Voting Rights Act?*

"Ain't you going to the army?" Gloria asked Milton.

"I'm going to college." Milton continued to talk and used the word oppression over and over. I kept my eye on Reubin. Gloria folded her arms over her chest and let out a deep breath, all the time watching the activity around the tables. Then out of the blue Milton said to me, "Little Sister, who in your family got raped by the white man?" I was startled by the question. *What is he talking about?* I was confused. He explained, "It's clear that you have white blood in you because of the way you look. You've got that straight hair and yellow skin."

"I don't have white blood. Or yellow skin" I snapped back. My skin was simply nice and tanned from the summer sun.

"It's alright. You don't have to get mad. Elijah Muham-mad will tell you that it is not your fault. Somebody back in your family's history had white blood raped into their veins.

I could not take any more of Milton's talking. I felt antsy and all flushed red in the face from the heat and from what Milton was saying. "I'm getting food." I slid myself off the steps and thought *Milton is one strange dude.*

"Me too." Gloria slid off the seat after me. I knew that I looked like my Cherokee grandmother and from all I knew my granddaddy did not rape her. But I did file away what he said about rape in my family and determined that I would ask my mother about it one day.

∞

I helped myself to a chicken drumstick, green beans and a small piece of corn bread that was still resting in a hot cast iron frying pan. The chicken was tender and tangy.

Someone tuned the radio to the Charlotte station and increased the volume. The Isley Brothers were singing "*It's your thing. Do what you want to do.*"Folks smiled, talked, ate and laughed. Then I walked straight toward the table where Reuben Martinez was sitting. When he saw me coming toward the table, he stood up. At that, I almost changed my direction. I avoided Reuben's eyes and helped myself to the macaroni and cheese sitting next to him on the table. After taking the noodles, I glanced sideways to my left to see that Reuben was looking at me.

"Chug makes some good macaroni and cheese. You want to make sure to have some of this." I smiled into Reuben's eyes, then looked at my plate.

"I'll make sure to have some."

I picked at the food with my fork for a few seconds.

"Where you from?"

Reuben made room for me next to him on the bench. "San Fernando Valley. Near Los Angeles, California." Reuben's accent set him apart from everyone. He sounded like Ricky from the *I Love Lucy Show*. I happily sat down.

California and the sound of Reuben's other words grabbed my full attention. I had thought about Los Angeles and Hollywood, California, many times before. The beaches from Frankie Avalon movies and the things that the Beach Boy sang about; surfing, California girls, everything. "Wow, do you live near the ocean?"

190

"Not that far. Me and my friends use to jump in the car and go over the hill into Los Angeles and go down to Venice Beach on Sundays."

"Your family lives back there?"

"Yes, lots of aunts and uncles and cousins."

"You must miss it? Them? California." I was star struck just being that close to someone that lived where movie stars live. "Do you go to Hollywood?"

"Yeah. Sure. I go to Hollywood. It's not that special."

"It must be."

We went on about California, Hollywood, Malibu beach, and Los Angeles for a long time. By the time I threw my paper plate into the trash barrel, Reuben and I had migrated to the edge of the yard away from the rest of the crowd. He seemed like a nice person and I thought that he might have stayed quiet if I had not asked him questions.

"How old are you?" He seemed my own age.

"Nineteen. How old are you?

"My birthday is in three months and I'll be fourteen." He looked off into the field when I said my age as though he was looking for someone from his past there. "Are you going to Vietnam?"

Reuben's search for someone in the field changed to a deflated expression. His face lost whatever life it had acquired during the moments of our conversation. "Yes, that's what we are preparing for now. We're doing maneuvers in the woods to get ready."

"In our woods?" I looked around at the wooded areas and imagined all the soldiers with their helmets and guns tromping through the pines and the oaks, down by the branch and by the sawdust piles. I had no idea that our woods could be so important as to be worth having soldiers train in them to go to Vietnam. Reuben's expression changed again. A far away look replaced the sadness. I wondered if he wanted to be somewhere else or was not looking forward to going to Vietnam, or both. I changed the subject. "We don't have any Reuben Martinezes around here. What is it?"

"A name." He smiled at me.

"No. What are you?

"A man." Another smile.

"You know what I mean." I smiled too. "What kind of name is Reuben Martinez?"

"I'm Puerto Rican."

"Puerto Rican? Does that mean you came from Puerto Rico?" Reuben explained to me about the people of Puerto Rico being a mixture of races and about his family moving to the Valley when he was young. His face livened again as he told me about all the times he's had with his family members who joined together for parties and celebrations. I liked Reuben Martinez and I decided that I wanted to go to California one day to be around people that were something different than just black or just white. I wanted to see all those people together that were a mix of other races.

I wanted to talk with Reuben for longer, but Lee and the other boys joined us and moved the conversation to basic training and army pay. I rejoined Gloria who was talking with her girl cousin, but my thoughts stayed with Reuben Martinez and his Puerto Rican family.

∞

On the Sunday evening after meeting Reuben at Gloria's house, and back at Mrs. Richardson's, I settled in to watch the Ed Sullivan Show with her in her bedroom. During commercials, sweater draped over her shoulders, she read the Sunday paper through her gray-rimmed glasses.

As we waited for the special tribute to Robert F. Kennedy to come back on, Mrs. Richardson dropped her hands holding the newspaper down into her lap. "Now the colored want to join the Miss America pageant." I looked at her. "Each race should have their own. Keep it separate." Just as sudden as she had dropped her hands and the paper into her lap, she lifted the paper again and continued reading.

My brow crinkled. I thought about Reuben's mixed race Puerto Rican people.

"Which pageant should Puerto Ricans be in?" I asked in the same quick, matter-of-fact way as she had made her comment.

"Puerto Ricans? What?" Mrs. Richardson seemed perplexed by my question.

"Puerto Ricans are black and white."

"Puerto Ricans are Asian!" With that explanation, Mrs. Richardson returned to reading.

"But."

With eyes still on the paper, she said, "But what?"

"But they're a mixture of black and white."

Mrs. Richardson seemed uninterested in my words. With images of blacks and whites mingling together in my mind, she looked at me and said, "You're going with me to Whispering Pines next weekend. Betty is coming down for a golf tournament and we're invited to go stay with them."

I felt an odd mixture of excitement about traveling with Mrs. Richardson to Whispering Pines to visit her millionaire daughter's second home and unease about the mixing of races that was both prohibited and a reality in the world.

21

Mrs. Richardson and I drove through Pinehurst and Southern Pines on our way to Whispering Pines. The summer's sun-toasted-pine-needle smell came in through the Saratoga's air vents.

The hour-long drive evoked the customary longer-than-an-hour feeling when going to a new place. Every house, every store, every field and every stand of trees took special interest in my mind. Associations arose for each thing, place, and person along the way. It took tolerance of great mental activity to go to a new place.

We entered the Whispering Pines community late morning. Mrs. Richardson said that her daughter had arrived the night before from Richmond and would have had the house opened and aired by the time we arrived.

My thoughts raced with private questions. *What did a millionaire look like? How did one act? Did they give money away? Was a wife millionaire different than the husband millionaire?* Mrs. Richardson had said that Betty's husband, Herbert, had made his fortune from the Dixie Container Corporation. "He is the person responsible for the paper cup you use when you brush your teeth," she had told me. I supposed he had made a great many of those cups and other things to have made a million dollars from them. "Betty and Herbert live in a mansion in Richmond." Mrs. Richardson had said. "Betty comes to their golf house more often than Herbert. He's so busy."

I had not seen a whole community just for playing golf before. I heard the pines swooshing around. The sunshine shone in through the tall trees and lit portions of driveways, yards and homes that we passed. There were two-story houses and one-story houses. There were large homes and smaller ones. Every home had a neat yard and pine trees. The toasty smell of dry pine needles, the air swooshing around gently, the sunshine, the houses amongst the pines, and the lake made me feel as special as an angel on a cloud. Macy, Mrs. Richardson's other daughter that lived in Troy, had a house in Whispering Pines too. We were going to see her later.

I liked Macy and I was looking forward to meeting Betty. They both had children who were grown. Even though Macy was not a millionaire like Betty, she was beautiful and nice. I wondered if Betty was going to be like her sister or whether a million dollars made you different than other people.

"Here it is," Mrs. Richardson made a left turn into a driveway that led to a ranch style house. The roof was clay red and the house a pale yellow. Portions of the front of the house had columns of red and earth-toned bricks. The entryway into the house had a high roof over it and a very large door with windows as tall on each side.

Mrs. Richardson shut off the engine and tooted her horn two quick times. "Lets get the bags." I helped her find her purse, and I watched as she checked herself in the mirror. She pressed lipstick-covered lips together before climbing out of the car. I stood beside her as she opened the trunk with her key.

As I pulled the three bags from the trunk, the front door of the house swung open. "Hi Mother." The voice was lilting. The red-haired, slim woman's house slippers emoted an air squishing sound followed by little clops as she walked toward us. Mrs. Richardson turned and walked in a controlled manner toward her daughter. The two women wrapped one arm each around the other and rather than kissing on the cheeks made kissing sounds into the air as they touched cheek to cheek. "You look good, Mother." Betty looked her mother over from head to toe as if making notes about her conservative styled grey hair, the tan knit skirt suit that she wore, her neutral colored pumps and the purse that hung from her arm.

Mrs. Richardson turned to me. "Levonne, you can bring one of the bags and then come back and get the rest." Betty took the five or so steps toward me. She looked older than I had expected she would look. Her face was pretty but not as pretty as her sister Macy's. She made quick dainty steps when she walked. Her walk said *I am a one hundred percent confident female.*

"Hi Levonne. I'm Betty. Let me take that."

"No Betty. Don't lift that. Levonne can get it."

"Oh Mother. I can carry it."

I followed behind Mrs. Richardson and Betty as the older woman continued to insist that Betty not burden herself with a suitcase. Betty's fingernails and toenails were manicured and were covered with a subdued reddish-colored nail polish.

The slight fragrances left behind by the older and younger woman ahead of me, the smell of the lake, and the loud chirps and pitches of birds that darted around the front yard made me wonder if I had arrived in heaven.

∞

"What do you want to order Levonne?" Macy laid her menu on the table.

"Ah..."

"You can take your time to decide. Do you need any help?"

I shook my head and read from the two pages of food items. It was my first experience choosing from a menu in a sit-down restaurant. The light, the deep reds and silvers of the room distracted me. The table's place settings were laid out before us. A waitress delivered glasses of water with ice. Beads of sweat rolled down the sides of the glasses. I sat across from Macy. Betty sat across from her mother. The restaurant was half filled with people–dressed in the knits and cotton casual wear that I had quickly come to associate with playing the game of golf.

Pastrami sandwiches, clubs, bacon, lettuce and tomato. I finally decided on a hamburger.

"Take a child out to eat and they will inevitably order a hamburger. Betty Lee and Hudgie used to always order a hamburger, no matter where we went when they were little," Betty said.

I was glad to know that I was normal in my selection. As normal as the children from Betty's life. That made me relaxed and happy to have done the right thing. I liked being with the millionaire, her mother, and the millionaire's sister. I felt as though I fit right in until Mrs. Richardson started with her stories.

"Levonne is as strong as an ox. I tell her to haul a load of rocks off and she does exactly as I say. Levonne tells me 'yessum, Mrs. Richardson.'"

At the word 'yessum,' Macy gives a sucking click with her tongue, jerks her head and looks at me for an instant and reprimands her mama, "Mother, Levonne doesn't talk like that!"

Macy's words did not stop Mrs. Richardson from going on with the story, "You should see how much she can carry." It was true what Macy asserted. I had never used the word *yessum* my entire childhood. In fact Mrs. Richardson was the only real person I ever heard say the word.

∞

The rest of the time at Whispering Pines I spent driving the golf cart up and down Betty's driveway, sitting on the pier out back of Macy's house, and eating good food with every meal that Betty or Macy prepared. The one chore I did was washing dishes after meals. Mrs. Richardson and I had had our first vacation together, and it was perfect. I felt like one of the family.

∞

Back home in Mrs. Richardson's living room, as I looked at the covers of her *Reader's Digest* hardback books in her bookcase cabinet, she walked in and said in a surprised tone, "Levonne, you can go anywhere as long as you keep your mouth shut." At the time, I did not know that my speech was so like the blacks I had lived and gone to school with most of my life. Nor did I appreciate the implications of the associations that my voice made in the ears of whites. But Mrs. Richardson said I could go anywhere. Just remember to keep my mouth shut. "In a few years, when you have your driver's license, you can drive us all over the country." Mrs. Richardson seemed excited and happy.

"You mean we could drive to your daughter's in Florida?" I had been dreaming of going to Florida since Mrs. Richardson went there and came back with pamphlets of Weeki Wakki Mermaid World and Busch Gardens with all the pink flamingos.

"Yes, and Richmond too. We could go out to Tennessee to see my sister."

Tennessee, Virginia, Florida. I was thrilled. I was going to see the world driving Mrs. Richardson in her turquoise and white Saratoga.

22

Following my trip to Whispering Pines and Mrs. Richardson's declaration of our future travel plans, I wanted to go to Dunn-Green Town to tell everyone. As I rode my bicycle down the road from the white part of Star to the black section, I recalled the lake, the golf cart that I drove, going out to eat at a nice restaurant and having the same thing that a millionaire's child ordered. I imagined driving a highway into big cities with Mrs. Richardson beside me, shopping at big department stores and eating at whatever restaurant we chose along the way.

When I walked into my parents' home through the standing-open front door, there sat my father in a straight backed chair. He looked at me with the distressed eyes of a sick person. He quaked all over. Streams of sweat rolled down his face. "Your mama 'as left me." I looked down at my father. I had no idea that someone leaving another person could have such a physical effect. I felt sorry for him. The man who walked through life without apology for anything, sat cowering over being left by a wife that he was often aggressive toward.

"She's gone?" I questioned my father's message and scanned for my brothers' presence in the house.

"She's at Annie's." Another tremble passed through his body.

"When did she leave?"

"Yesterday." He took his time saying the word as if a rib was broken and sticking into his side.

"Where's Lee?"

"We got to get her back."

As I walked the path between my parents' and the neighbor's houses, I felt a new sense of power. Leaving someone could change their personality. I rejoiced in my mother's action against my father's drunken verbal and physical attacks. He needed to be taught a lesson.

∞

In Gloria's backyard, eight Dunn-Green boys, including my three brothers, stood around an army truck. Nobody seemed to notice my approach except one of the passengers. Reuben Martinez.

Upon seeing me, Reuben opened the door and stepped out of the truck, causing the boys to spread like ants having a stick drawn through their line.

"Que paso?" Reuben said to me.

"What?" I laughed at the word.

"What's happening? Que paso?"

I laughed again and repeated the word. "What is that?"

"It's Spanish," he explained. I was impressed by how different Reuben was from anyone else that I had known. He had an unusual name and he could speak another language

"So you speak Spanish?"

"Hablo espanol todos anos."

"Wow. What does that mean?

He laughed. "I knew Spanish before I knew English."

Remembering that Mrs. Richardson called Puerto Ricans Asian, I asked, "Are you Asian?"

Reuben laughed again. "You have lots of questions."

"I was just wondering."

"Some Puerto Ricans are part Asian. But we're not Asian."

"What are your parts?"

"Probably a lot like yours." I listened but didn't speak. "You're part white and black."

"And Cherokee Indian."

"And so am I." My eyes widened. "Well, not Cherokee but some kind of American Indian. But we don't break it down all the time like you all do here in the states. We're just Puerto Rican." I thought that it must be nice to be Puerto Rican and just be everything, without having to think about it. I told Reuben that one day I was going to drive out to California and when I did, I was going to look him up. He laughed. "I better give you my address then." He pulled a short pencil from his pocket and a piece of paper and wrote down two addresses. One, he explained, was an army address where I could send letters and the other, his parents' house in California. I put the paper in my pocket with every intention of writing to him.

The truck engine fired and Reuben told me good-bye and

climbed back in. We all watched as the trunk sprang over the ruts in the road leading away from Gloria's house.

In her kitchen, I found six-year-old Frankie sitting at their table eating a biscuit with Welch's grape jelly. His clothes were dirty and his feet shoeless. When he saw me, his face lit up and he gave me his usual big hug. Bernice said, "Looks like somebody loves his sister."

"Hey," I said to Bernice and then to Gloria.

"What you up to, Miss Levonne?" Bernice asked.

"Just came home to visit for a while."

"Your mama done left your daddy, huh?"

"Yes ma'am. He's not doing too great either."

"Serves him right. He don't treat Ovella the way a man should."

Gloria and I listened as Bernice went on about how my mama had done the right thing to leave. I wondered how long she would be gone, because I realized that someone had to take care of Frankie. While sitting there listening, I decided that I would take him back with me to Mrs. Richardson's.

∞

The woman that I lived with, upon realizing that I'd brought my brother back to her house to stay, was not receptive to the idea.

"Oh no, we can't have him here."

"But Mama's gone and Daddy is not in any kind of shape to take care of him."

"What about your brother? Lee? Can't he take care of him?"

204

I wanted to tell Mrs. Richardson that Lee would not take care of Frankie the way that I would or could. I wanted to tell her that I would make sure that my brother was no trouble to her, but Frankie was already plucking off the roses beside the carport. Mrs. Richardson said, "No. No Frankie. You can't touch the roses." Then to me she said, "He can't stay here. He can spend the night, but he has to go home tomorrow." She looked Frankie over and added, "You have to clean him up if he's going to be in the house." Mrs. Richardson took a seat on the front porch with her newspaper. "Take his things out of that bag and shake them, and the bag, well before you take them into the house. Cock roaches love paper bags."

Three t-shirts, a pair of pants, socks, underwear. I shook each thing, one piece of clothing at a time. Then I shook the bag. No roaches. I gave my brother his first bath in a bathtub, then cleaned it out with Comet as Mrs. Richardson had directed me to do after every use. I had a good time showing Frankie around the basement, the back yard and the pond out by the Russell Mansion. I loved watching Frankie have a good time.

∞

The next day while Mrs. Richardson was at church, I showed Frankie around the inside of Mrs. Richardson's house. But first I had to break in, because she had locked me out of all but my room again.

First I showed Frankie what was in the attic. "Crawl, Frankie. Put your weight on the wood." I did not want him to step between the joists and go through the ceiling. We looked in boxes at Mrs. Richardson's youngest son's things from the dental school that she told me she regretted him not finishing. There were small metal picks and a mold for teeth. There were books and papers with words on them that were foreign to me.

After the attic, I showed Frankie the organ and we played on it for a while before I took him back to Dunn-Green Town.

23

Mrs. Richardson removed a can of pork and beans from the cabinet, walked the few steps to the electric can opener, situated the can just right against the magnet and pressed the mechanism that activated the lid cutting. I felt sadness and concern as I held a picture of Frankie in my mind. I could see him seated before the bookcase that Lee made in industrial arts class, looking at pictures in the encyclopedia. I hoped somebody was looking after him. The can top clicked several times as the can opener completed its task. Mrs. Richardson said, "We're going to Virginia next week."

"Virginia?" I felt my eyelids stretch wide open. "Next week?"

She reached into a lower cabinet and pulled out a pot. "We'll stay with my son Roy and his wife in Newport News. He lives on the Chesapeake Bay." *A bay?* The name Chesapeake Bay sounded wonderful. I imagined ships coming in from foreign ports. Mrs. Richardson spooned the beans into the pot. "We'll stay at Roy's for a few days, then we'll go to Betty's in Richmond."

My smile was so full that I felt the glow of it radiate throughout my entire body. I wanted to jump up and down and clap my hands. "Wow." I thought about what I would take with me on the trip.

Mrs. Richardson looked at me and chuckled a bit as she clicked a burner knob of the stove into the low heat position. She took another pot from a lower cabinet. "Get yourself a hot dog." I took a frozen wiener from the packet in the freezer and popped it in the pot of water. "Maybe we'll go to Virginia Beach while we're up there."

"The beach!" I stood in all my joy. Hands over my mouth. *The beach and the millionaire's house too* I said to myself. Mrs. Richardson retrieved from the refrigerator a left over piece of steak from her dinner the night before and placed it in the toaster oven. She walked out of the kitchen. I had to tell someone right away.

∞

In my room, I took a pen from my vanity cabinet drawer and a notebook from the closet. From my clothing drawer, I took the piece of paper with Reuben Martinez's addresses on it. His image formed in my mind.

—

July 20, 1968

Dear Reuben,

How much longer will you be doing maneuvers in Star? When are you leaving for Vietnam? I'll write to you while you're there. And when you return and are back with your family in California and when I am eighteen, I plan to come see you there.

Do you remember I said that I live with an old white woman? She is the one who took me to Whispering Pines, the golfing place. Well, now she is going to take me to Virginia. We will go to Newport News on the Chesapeake Bay first to see her son, then we will go see her millionaire daughter that lives in Richmond. (This is the same daughter that has a house in Whispering Pines.)

I am excited about this trip because we will also go to Virginia Beach and I have never seen the ocean before. Maybe when I come out to California, I can go with you to see your ocean. That would be really great.

Maybe I will see you before I take the trip or maybe it will be after we get back in two weeks. I am looking forward to seeing you again. Maybe next time we are together, we could take a walk. I could show you the pond where I used to go fishing. You pass it, though you don't see it, from the road on your way into Dunn-Green Town. Well, I will close for now.

Love,

Levonne

—

Before I could reread what I had written to Reuben, Mrs. Richardson called, "come get your lunch." I folded the letter and tucked it under my clothing in my bottom drawer.

∞

Mrs. Richardson's son Roy in Newport News was very nice. He drove me in his truck to my first dock. "You carry this." Roy, who was about fifty years old and did not have any children of his own, handed me a cage that he called a crab pot. As we walked on the black asphalt toward the bay with many docks and boats, seagulls called as they flew overhead. Men, some with children, passed us, carrying small chests of fishing gear and fishing rods. The sunshine and warm moist air that surrounded us felt like an extension of my body. It was a perfect temperature. Roy looked at my hands and said, "You take good care of your fingernails." I looked at my hands too. My nails were shiny from the clear nail polish that I had put on them several days before.

"Yes sir." I had never had a grown man or even a boy for that matter notice my fingernails nor say anything about them. I could tell from the way Roy sounded that he was impressed. I felt proud.

The long wooden dock stretched out in front of us. It was grayed from the weather. "We're going to toss in down there." He pointed toward the end of the dock. The boards clanked and creaked beneath our feet as we walked the yards to the end.

"What are those?" The water was sprinkled with white floating creatures the sizes of golf and tennis balls.

"Jelly fish."

"I have heard of jelly fish." I stopped and watched the jelly fish float and move about in the water.

"They can sting you. You don't want to touch one."

I was amazed at the abundance of jelly fish in the water. I wondered how they coexisted with the other animals and fish. Whether they stung them also.

At the end of the dock, Roy attached pieces of raw chicken to the inside wall of the crab pot, then closed the trap door. On a light-weight, plastic-like rope, he lowered the trap beneath the jelly fish. The trap dropped out of sight, and Roy tied the rope to a pier post. "Let's go fish. We'll check this later." I was excited and could not wait to see what we would catch in the trap.

Roy and I took folding chairs from the bed of his pickup and sat in a grassy area near the dock. We fished with rods while we talked and drank sodas.

"What grade are you in?"

"I'm in high school next year."

"Are you looking forward to that?"

"Yes, I get to see friends from the school I used to go to."

"Oh? What school was that?" He looked at me when he asked.

"Brutonville. I went there through the sixth grade, and I changed schools and went to a school in Star. That's when I started staying with Mrs. Richardson." I tossed the line from the rod once more into the water.

"How was the school in Star?" Roy continued to look at me. At the time I knew nothing about the bitter fight against desegregation of schools in his area.

"It was alright." I usually said something good to adults about things in my life because my mama had always said that if you can't say something good about a thing, don't say anything at all.

"What did you like most in school last year?"

I thought for a while. "I liked the field trip that Mr. Ray, our science teacher, took us on to Uwharrie Rock Quarry. I found rocks for a collection." Roy seemed impressed. He asked questions about the different kinds of rocks. I shared with him how my favorites were micas because they were so unusual with their flakey makeup and their translucent color. I explained about pyrite and muscovite and how I preferred the muscovite just because of its name.

"Do you have a best friend?"

I thought about my friendless time at Star Elementary the past few years. "Teresa was my best friend."

"She's not anymore?"

"Her mother was my fourth grade teacher. She had to leave Brutonville because her mama got a job somewhere else."

"Oh?"

"I haven't made a new best friend since then."

"Well, you're a smart girl and pretty, too. I know that you'll have a best friend again." Roy listened to my stories in a way that no grown man had ever listened to me before. I liked him and thought Mrs. Richardson was pretty lucky to have such a very nice son.

We caught enough crabs in the crab trap for a dinner. It was a little freaky to watch Roy's wife, Marie, cook the live crabs in a big pot of hot water. But the meat was delicious dipped in melted butter. Roy and Marie were really nice people.

∞

Before we left Newport News, Marie took me and Mrs. Richardson to Virginia Beach for the day. We had to first buy me a bathing suit so that I could get into the water. Marie and Mrs. Richardson waited and watched on the boardwalk while I went to the water and had some fun in the waves.

I was intimidated at first by all the people that I did not know and the roar of the waves smashing in against the shore. But I figured that if the little kids could go out and play in the waves, I sure could, too. Not knowing how to swim, I did not go where the water was deeper than knee level. I had a ton of fun. I wished Frankie or Teresa, heck, even Reuben, could be with me. But alone, I still had a very great time. Me and Mrs. Richardson were having a second vacation together that summer and it was working out fabulously.

∞

Betty and Betty's black maid met us at the front door of her Richmond, Virginia mansion. After hellos and watching Mrs. Richardson and her daughter hug, the maid took me and my bag to the room where I would sleep. We walked down a very elegant carpeted hallway that had large paintings on the walls, busts of what must have been famous people on shelves, and furniture for sitting even though it was just a hallway. We went past many doors that I longed to explore behind and into the kitchen area.

The kitchen was the size of half of Mrs. Richardson's house. From the kitchen, the maid took me down another hallway with three bedrooms, a bathroom and a washer and dryer. She showed me my room. It was nice. The floor was shiny and spotless. There were two twin beds in the room. The maid told me which one I could have.

After putting my clothes in the drawer like the maid told me, I made my way back down to the kitchen. Everything seemed spacious. The maid washed vegetables at the sink.

I walked to the windows and looked out over a swimming pool that reflected blue light onto everything. The shrubs and trees around the rear of the house, far beyond the perimeter of the pool, all looked neatly manicured.

"Want something to drink?"

"Yes ma'am." I was delighted to have a maid asking me if I wanted something to drink, but I also felt guilty having her wait on me. "Thank you," I said when the maid sat a bottle of cold Coca Cola along with a glass of ice on the table with six chairs around it. I sat down and studied the blue and white reflections off the pool.

"What grade you in at school?"

"Ninth grade."

"High school. You like going to school down in North Carolina?"

"Yes ma'am."

"You got a lot of friends?"

"Yes ma'am. I have lots of friends that I'll be seeing that I haven't seen since sixth grade."

"Well that's good."

We chatted on about me having family in North Carolina, me staying with Mrs. Richardson. How it started out just as a summer thing and now I was with her for the second summer. I told the maid how we were going to drive all over the country once I had my driver's license and how Mrs. Richardson was just like family to me.

"Uh huh. That's why you staying back here. 'Cause you family."

I didn't understand what the maid was telling me back

then because I still was not clear about the difference between being family and a servant. I had no idea about the reason Mrs. Richardson told me not to go wondering around the house, but to stay in the bedroom or in the kitchen area with the maid. I was not aware of the clear distinction between the help's place and the bosses' domain. But I did know that I was bored looking at *Life* and *Look* magazines at the table in the kitchen and looking at the little television in my room for two whole days. I was very pleased when Mrs. Richardson said we were going into the city to see her sister.

∞

Richmond was the most beautiful city. Big trees with limbs hanging out over city streets. Lots of shade and sprinkled sun light. Two-storied houses standing side by side down the streets with cars parked along it. The houses were all unique. A different color, different windows, different decorative trim. "My sister runs a boarding house for men." Mrs. Richardson's sister's house was beautiful. Dark green, two stories high with lots of big windows all around. Her porch had a wide berth of steps leading to a porch with many outdoor chairs and sofas for sitting and enjoying the evening's pleasures.

Inside was a large living room filled with comfortable looking chairs, a dining room with a table big enough to seat sixteen people, a buffet beside the table, and a very big kitchen with several workers bustling around. Mrs. Richardson's sister seemed in a hurry, tending to this and calling for that. She was distracted during the time she sat with us to have a cup of tea. Sending people here and there to do one thing or another made her one busy woman, even busier than Mrs. Richardson.

When I started up her set of carpeted stairs with the wooden hand rails on both sides, she said, "Even I don't go up there. You wouldn't want to know what you might find. Only men live there." I looked at the stairs and wished more than ever that I could explore and experience what it was that Mrs. Richardson's sister said that I would not want to see. She did not understand that I wanted to see everything and know everything. But since it was her house and since I did not have time to wait for the right moment to sneak up those stairs, I had to leave her fine boarding house unexplored.

Mrs. Richardson later said that her sister had needed a better husband, so she would not have to work so hard for the rest of her life. I know for one thing that I would love to live with Mrs. Richardson's sister for a while and help her out at her place.

Visiting Mrs. Richardson's sister was the last thing we did in Virginia. The next day we went back home to North Carolina, but not before spending another night at Betty's house where all I saw was the kitchen, ate with the maid, and didn't even go outside to look around. I wondered what good it was to go to a millionaire's house if all you could do was look at magazines. I much preferred my time at Roy's house.

24

Standing at the bottom of the steps into my parents' house, before I climbed the first one, I could hear that things were right back where they had been before my Mama left Daddy trembling in the straight-backed chair weeks before. Daddy was stomping around the house talking about what my mama was not doing that he was mad about. I entered. Mama was folding clothes on the couch and smoking a cigarette.

"Hey," I said to anybody that had the time of day for me.

Daddy was quiet. He looked at me and said, "Hey. How you doing?"

"Just fine," I told him. But that was before what was going on began spoiling the feelings I had from my trip to Virginia. "Hey Mama," I said as I sat down on the other side of the pile of clothes and began folding.

"What you doing home?" I could tell that Mama was still thinking about my daddy but was trying to give me some attention too.

"Me and Mrs. Richardson just came back from Virginia."

"Virginia? What y'all do in Virginia?"

"We stayed with her son Roy and then with her millionaire daughter, Betty. Mama, I went to Virginia Beach and swam in the ocean."

"I went to Virginia Beach once. It's nice up there."

Daddy tromped out the front door and I felt the freedom to ask my mother some questions. "Mama, did you stay at Aunt Annie's?" I asked more quietly.

Mama nodded and turned to look back at the door. "Your daddy sent for me and swore he'd stopped drinking and fighting."

"He's winding up. He ain't changed, Mama."

Mama looked anxious and puffed again on her cigarette. She looked at the door. Then she began folding one of Dale's t-shirts and placed it in a new pile. I folded my daddy's bandana handkerchief and put it in a pile Mama had already started. I wondered what on earth she was going to do.

∞

From the path leading to Gloria's, I saw my brothers horsing around with the boys from the neighborhood. Frankie ran circles around the group of them. On her porch, I passed Gloria's grandpa, who sat in a straight-backed chair looking out at the field of weeds. "How you, Mr. Will?"

"Doing alright, Child." He propped his arms on the top of a cane that he used to help him get around.

Ms. Lily sat in the living room fanning and singing church songs out loud. She nodded her head at me when I entered the house and paused in her singing long enough to say, "How you, Honey?" in a melodic voice. I said I was fine and walked on through to the kitchen.

Gloria stood behind Bernice's chair fanning a hot comb in the air. "How y'all doing?"

"Hey Girlie. I'm getting' ready to go out tonight. Gloria, hurry up and get done with my hair. I got things to do before the sun goes down."

"Hey." Gloria smiled and pulled the hot iron through a small section of Bernice's hair.

"Me and Mrs. Richardson just got back from Virginia."

"Y'all doing some traveling? What all did you see?" Bernice asked as she winced from the heat of the comb close to her scalp. I told them about fishing with Roy in Chesapeake Bay, visiting a boarding house in Richmond and about the millionaire's house, but how I stayed in the kitchen most of the time and talked to the maid.

"She had you hanging out with the maid, did she?" Bernice laughed. "She's trying to school you, Child. Get you ready."

I did not like Bernice's words. I felt my anger stir.

I returned the conversation to crab pots and how we inadvertently caught jelly fish and star fish along with the crabs. I told them how crab meat tastes and how pleasing Roy and his wife were to visit, but underneath I still felt bugged by Bernice's servant insinuation.

As I talked, Gloria went to the window and looked outside to investigate the sound of engine noise. "It's Jerry and another soldier," she said. I joined Gloria at the window. We watched. Two soldiers sat in the front seats. I felt immediate excitement.

Gloria reported, "Reuben too."

Bernice teased, "Girl, that Reuben been down here three times this week asking 'bout Levonne." Gloria looked at me and giggled. "Honey, you got yourself a boyfriend," Bernice nodded her head at me. "You sure have. Come on back here and get my hair finished, Girl." Gloria took her position behind Bernice and continued with the job. "Go on out. You know you want to see him."

"Yeah," Gloria added.

Outside, I joined Reuben and Jerry by the jeep. "Hey." Ruben shut the jeep door behind him and wore a big smile.

"Hey. I wrote you a letter to tell you about my travels."

"Travels?"

"Yeah. But I didn't mail it yet. I've been to Newport News and Richmond, Virginia. And Virginia Beach too."

Reuben and I walked to the playground out of sight of Gloria's house and sat on the old weathered picnic bench.

"We're leaving soon."

I felt disappointment right away. "Leaving?"

"Some of us are going to Vietnam and some of us are going to Korea."

"Korea? Is there a war in Korea too?"

"No, but there was."

"Which one will you go to?"

"They haven't told us yet.

"Well, I hope you're going to where there's no war." I already missed Reuben. "When do you go?"

"They ship us out in a week or so. I might not know where I'm going or even exactly when I'm going 'til the day we leave."

I looked at the fields that surrounded the playground. As I wondered what was to come of me and Reuben Martinez, Lee approached from the direction of Gloria's house. "When I finish high school, I'm coming to see you in California," I said. The crunch of Lee's shoes on the rocky dirt road became louder. I asked, "Will you write me back?"

I could not hear Reuben's response as Lee's words interrupted us. "Daddy said come home!" Lee had never come for me with a message from home in our entire lives before. I thought it weird and proceeded to ignore him. I continued talking with Reuben. Lee said a second time. "I told you that Daddy wants you home. Now! He's serious. You better come." I ignored Lee and his directions and watched as he left stating, "I told you."

Lee's second visit ten minutes later came as a bigger surprise than his first visit. He repeated our father's command for me to return home. I told Reuben, "I better go." He stood and looked at me in a way that said he wished I did not have to.

"Hey are you going to be around this week?"

"I don't know," I said. "Maybe tomorrow?"

"I'll come back to see you."

As I left with Lee, Reuben watched. Gloria tossed a pan of dish water from her back porch. The tension of my situation made me crave company. "Gloria. Walk with me home." Lee, after a brief pause, walked away without speaking.

"Give me a minute." Gloria went back inside and as I waited, Reuben caught up with me. There in Gloria's backyard, with only him and me present, Reuben pulled me to

221

him by my shoulders. "I like you," he told me and then he kissed me, first lightly on my mouth, then again, more firmly. I felt a warm wave of sensation that started in my lower torso and spread throughout my entire body. My heart thumped so strongly that I was sure he could see it beating. My body, drawn like a magnet to him, squeezed itself against his body. I felt some kind of wonderful in Reuben's princely embrace.

"I'm ready." Gloria's voice startled me. I jumped, then laughed along with Reuben. I stepped away from the soldier with whom I thought I might be in love, grabbed Gloria by her arm, and the two of us walked off.

On the path between Gloria's house and my family's, we walked over broken rock embedded in red soil. We chatted in one continuous stream of intermingled voices the entire two or three minutes from her house to mine, about Reuben Martinez and going to California to see him one day and how maybe she would go on the trip with me.

As Gloria and I prepared to climb the steps to my front door, we stopped at the sounds of my father's raised voice. "Where is she?" I heard Lee mumble a response. "Goddammit, I don't want to have to go down there myself!" Daddy's work boots thumped hard against the linoleum-covered floor as he moved at a pace quicker than his normal pace toward the door.

Gloria turned away from me so quickly that I did not have time to formulate words after her. I watched her flee around the corner of our house, leaving me standing alone to face this man who at the moment seemed more a puzzle to me than a threat.

"Get in here." Daddy stood in the doorway of the living room and looked out at me. I climbed the steps and brushed past my father. Body sweat and alcohol smells filled my nose. I looked at the floor. I felt naked in the moment that my father stared at me. "I know what that soldier's up to!" My father's voice increased in volume. A glance at his face disclosed his seriousness. The skin between his brows wrinkled, his eyes squinted, and his mouth moved, his body swayed as his arms made jerking motions. I told myself not to move and not to say a word, but my mind went to a place I had not needed to go before.

I registered the man, my father, the one I had counted on never to be aggressive toward me, even if he was toward others, including my mother. I felt my body stiffen and my lips harden. He was being possessive and he was wound tight. I made a decision as I watched him excite himself with talk about soldiers and his knowledge of a boy's intentions. The air surrounding him was *Tasmanian-devil* crazy. His crazy overtook me.

At that moment, standing there with my mad daddy, I made a decision. One aggressive hand on me was all it was going to take for me to do one of two things—get the hell out of there and never come back again or shoot the bastard standing before me. The fact that I did not have a gun for shooting was meaningless. I felt for the first time a fury toward my father that consumed my entire being.

As my mother watched from a passive position behind

the raging man and as Lee watched from his seat before the television, I saw my options clearly. I would hit the road, fly the coop, catch a bus out of Star or, if need be, I'd shoot Daddy if he turned on me as violently as he turned on Mama. I would not take my father's abuse.

And then he did it. He touched me. He shoved my shoulder. "You better listen to me." That touch was enough. I stomped out of the house, hopped on my bicycle and pedaled out of there, determined in my mind never to set foot before him again. I wished he was dead.

25

I rode the bicycle at a wild pace all the way back to Mrs. Richardson's. Dr. Scarborough's many acres and home, the other Russell house with their two white columns out front, my classmates—Franklin and Randy's houses—I passed without notice. My anger at my father fueled my explosive ride.

As I approached Mrs. Richardson's, Bernice's words from earlier in the day intruded into my mind. She had inferred that Mrs. Richardson was training me to be her maid. "I am not her maid," I yelled out loud as I turned the bicycle into the driveway. I longed for my room so that I might dream of the day when I would go to California to be with Reuben.

∞

Mrs. Richardson met me as I entered from outside. She tossed folded paper onto the dressing table before me in my room. "What is this?" she insisted. I looked at the paper. *What is it?* I wondered. "An old white woman? An old white woman? Is that how you see me?"

I looked at the paper again. It was my letter to Reuben. I remained silent. I looked at Mrs. Richardson, then at the floor. I had not really seen her angry before.

"Who is that you're writing?" I said nothing. "Is that what you're doing when you go down there? Running with boys? With grown men? Soldiers?"

I fought inside myself between a sense of defeat and anger.

"There are no good men left in this world. You might as well get that clear in your head now." I looked at the woman before me, searching her eyes for the logic in what she was saying. "That's right! The last one died when my Foster passed away."

Foster had been Mrs. Richardson's husband. She seemed very serious about the point of her husband having been the last good man in the world. Even I who had limited experience knew that her opinion about the scarcity of good men had to be wrong. But I could also see that she believed what she was saying. For a moment my view of her softened. I felt sorry that she had lost her Foster.

"Men are no good. Do you hear me?"

"Yes Ma'am."

"All they do is chase after a female like a dog chasing a bitch in heat." She turned and stomped out of my room.

Wow, I thought. I could not believe what I heard come out of Mrs. Richardson's mouth. She left me reeling. I sat down on the bench in front of the dressing table. I wondered whether I was crazy. My thoughts raced. I concluded that Mrs. Richardson was crazy. I felt angry. *I have a right to like someone. What's wrong with her?* I fingered my very private letter to Reuben and felt shame over being compared to a bitch in heat and anger over Reuben being compared to a dog. Then I wondered how Mrs. Richardson wanted me to see her—if not the *old white woman with whom I lived and for whom I worked.*

∞

I listened, unnoticed, as Mrs. Richardson talked on the telephone later in the day with her sister from Tennessee. "Levonne has changed. She used to be so attentive. She runs into my heels with the grocery cart when we go shopping." I wondered to myself *Have I changed?*

∞

After my father's confrontation, I told myself that he did not deserve me as a daughter. I made up my mind again not to see him, even though it meant that I did not see Reuben Martinez before he left our town to go fight a war. I did not travel home to my parents' house for the rest of the summer.

Mrs. Richardson used every chance during those months to reinforce her statements that all men were worthless, except of course her precious dead Foster. I was sure that Mrs. Richardson was off her rocker. I was determined that I was going to have a husband one day and that my husband was going to be a good man, maybe *even better* than Foster had been. Although I did not see Reuben again, I remembered the kiss and nurtured the dream that I would visit him one day in California. From then on, I hid the letters that I wrote to him in a secret place in the basement.

26

The fall morning air was cool and moist from the previous night's rain. I walked from Mrs. Richardson's to Star Elementary, where I would catch the bus with the other high-school-aged kids to East Montgomery. On my first morning of being a high-schooler, I picked brown, yellow and red leaves still clinging to trees along my route. It had been over two years since I had last seen my friends from Brutonville Elementary. I could not wait to see them.

Having arrived at Star Elementary early, before all the kids or teachers had gathered to wait for buses or to lineup for homeroom, I waited patiently. I sat on the stoop that led into the front of the main building. Several of my classmates from Star passed by, giving brief, polite greetings. When the bus arrived that held my brothers and their neighbors from Dunn-Green Town, I stood and waited as kids filed off one by one. I had not seen my brothers for nearly two months, since I left my father as he demanded that I stay away from Reuben.

Lee exited first, then Frankie. Dale exited the bus after Gloria. There was a flurry of quick hellos before I took

Frankie from Lee and walked him to his first grade classroom.

I missed my brothers. But school would have to be the place where we connected.

∞

A sea of white kids, sprinkled with black faces, from eastern Montgomery County filed off the orange buses and into the high school's hallway by the administrative offices. Students took turns reading lists stating to whom they were to report for homeroom.

One by one I greeted old friends. Seeing each one made me feel happy and sad simultaneously, the way one feels when they encounter someone they have missed but are glad finally encounter. We examined one another from head to toe for changes from and similarities to our old selves. I was in homeroom with Deborah, Beverly and Avis. We walked to Mrs. Wilson's room together. I noticed that Ola Mae arrived also, along with some of her former friends from Brutonville.

Though I was glad to see my old friends, the presence of the Star kids inhibited me. My former friends were also distracted by the kids with whom they had spent the previous two years.

I had not talked with Ola Mae on the school bus from Star. In the classroom I said, "Hey. How're you?"

"Good." Ola Mae smiled. She looked fresh in a new dress.

"Glad to be back at school?"

"Naw." Ola Mae did not smile, but held an expression on her face that agreed with her emphatic expression of not being glad. I noticed that Avis and her twin sister Javis were talking and I had not spoken to Javis yet.

"Later," I told Ola Mae and was off to greet other kids that I had not seen during the previous two grades.

∞

After morning classes, in the expansive new cafeteria, the aroma of yeast bread and baked meat permeated the chorus of deep and high-pitched kids' voices. The sea of former eighth graders, white kids and a sprinkling of blacks from Star, Biscoe, Candor, Eagle Springs, Jackson Springs, and West End buzzed like bees at a hive.

At lunchtime on the first day of high school, I could not break myself from the previous two years' training. I stood in line atop a shiny linoleum floor with Ola Mae and followed her to a table. Though I saw Avis and Javis, Deborah and Beverly along with some other girls, I felt incapable of choosing to sit with them. It was like I was an automaton. *What if they think I'm weird?* I asked myself. I had waited so long to rejoin my friends.

For some moments, it seemed Ola Mae and I just had one another, although we sat with girls from Brutonville—Annie Wall, Priscilla and Nelda Legrande, Elaine Harris. They were kids that I had known since first grade. But they felt like strangers to me. Other former classmates from Brutonville sat together—Lorenza Townsend and Michael Perry. "They're playing football," someone at our table commented. As everyone ate their meatloaf and mashed potatoes, I wanted to ask *how was your time since you left Brutonville?* but could not say aloud. Some kids laughed, others talked, and some seemed as natural as ever in their interactions. Some spoke to the white kids that passed by as though they might be friends.

As we, members of the freshman class, finished our lunches in one section of the cafeteria; juniors entered and then proceeded with their trays to a different section of the cafeteria.

Lee was part of the junior class. I was proud of him. He talked in line with his friends, Jerry Stancil and the two Jameses. *They are handsome* I thought. The girls at my table commented on their striking appearances.

The kids at our table left in small groups. Ola Mae and I prepared to leave the table as the seniors formed a line outside of the cafeteria. When we rose, I felt as awkward as Ola Mae looked in front of all the students that I had known from Brutonville, and near those we had spent the previous two years with in Star.

After emptying our trays, Ola Mae and I took a position along the wall in the bathroom, both hesitant to exit into the world outside its doors. The ties had been broken, and I was not sure how to reconstitute the relationships I had known. Ola Mae and I talked and smiled at everyone who entered.

When Deborah came in, she said, "Hey Levonne. Have you heard from Teresa?"

I ached for Teresa's friendship in that moment. If she had been there, I knew that I would know what to do. But she was not there. "No, I haven't."

"Me either. I'm going out for basketball. How about you?"

"No," I said. The image of my body engaged in sports embarrassed me. It was the last thing I wanted to do.

When Deborah reached for the door, she asked, "You going outside?"

I looked at Ola Mae and felt a shiver of fear and guilt. *Am I going to leave her, alone, standing in the bathroom?* It was what I had waited for, to leave her and have my own friends again. So why did I hesitate? Deborah looked at Ola Mae and said, "You can come too."

"No thanks." Ola Mae shifted on her feet and turned away from me to the crowd of girls standing by the sinks. I walked to the bathroom door with Deborah, breathed a deep breath, and left Ola Mae and the self I had become over the past two years with her.

27

Deborah, Beverly, Avis and sometimes her twin Javis, and I gathered in the library during study hall hour. We filed into the room as though it were our own. Each of the girls was beautiful in her unique way. Deborah was dark-skinned with large dark eyes. Her hair was long and black. She was the anchor of the group, the strength. Avis was modern. She wore a short afro. Avis' twin Javis was not as concerned with the latest fad in clothes or hairstyle as her sister. But both of the twins were hipped and full of life. Beverly was tall and light-skinned, though not as light as I. She had dark brown eyes and long brown hair. She was the best follower in the group. I was the lightest complexioned of them all. Standing out with the straightest hair compared to all of their curls, and grey green eyes next to their brown ones. We were a pleasant mixture of shades, styles, personalities and academic aspirations.

∞

At one library meeting several weeks into the school semester, I learned for the first time since I had reconnected with my friends how they saw me.

Beverly, Deborah, Avis and I sat around a dark wooden

table in hard chairs. Adult library staff glanced in at us from the other side of the glass, content to let us have our separate lives from theirs. Other students were content to leave us to ourselves in the room separated by windows from the rest of the library. I felt independent and most whole with this cohort of girl classmates. We all opened books before us on the table to give the impression that we were focused on studies.

"The army camp is totally empty," Beverly shared with us. "You know a lot of them got girlfriends in Biscoe when they were here. One of them got a girl pregnant and now he's gone."

"Pregnant?" I asked. I imagined a most desolate situation for the girl left behind. I turned a page in my Algebra textbook.

"Yeah. She wanted him to marry her before he left, but he wouldn't."

"What's she going to do?" Deborah asked.

"Have the baby. What else can she do?"

I wondered when Reuben had left, where he was. I had not seen him again after that day that my father raged at me for talking with him. "I met one of the soldiers," I confessed. All eyes turned to me.

"What did he look like?" Beverly asked.

"He's Puerto Rican," I explained. "They are a mixed race of people."

"Tell us what he looked like." Beverly insisted.

"He's about my brother Lee's size. He's cute."

"Y'all get it on?" Avis wanted to know as she maintained

a serious and mature expression on her face. The other girls giggled and shuffled their books in front of them.

"No." I felt my face warm. "He was really nice. I'm going to see him in California when I turn eighteen and after he's back from Vietnam."

"If he gets back." Avis said.

"Don't say that."

"It's the truth. A lot of soldiers die over there," Deborah said.

Beverly added, "Yeah. What about those body counts on television?"

"Reuben will get back. He might not be in Vietnam. He might be in Korea where there is no war right now."

"Don't you know where he is?" asked Avis.

"No. I didn't get a letter yet."

Everyone was quiet, all probably thinking of someone they knew that they wished would make it back alive. "Boys have to go to college to stay out of the war," Avis explained. That was the same thing that Milton had told Gloria and me the previous summer. "My sister goes to college up north. She says there are a lot of guys in college now." Avis spoke often of her older sister.

"How does she pay for college?" I asked, perplexed by the idea of my peers' family members having the money to go to college.

"Yeah." Deborah chimed.

"It's no problem. If you can't afford tuition and housing, you qualify for financial aid. If you don't have money, you can get a student loan. You can get grants that you don't have to pay back." I was intrigued. It had never occurred to me that poor people had access to college. I thought it was something for the rich. "You can get a job on a work study program too."

In that moment, for the first time, college became an option for me. I had always assumed that I would get married and have kids, the same as my mother had. Deborah said, "I'm thinking about going."

Beverly spoke. "All y'all smarter than me. I wouldn't be able to get into college."

"You can," Avis said. "Just pass everything in high school and you'll be able to get into college."

"You mean you don't have to make all A's?" Beverly seemed amazed.

"No, my sister made C's." We soaked in what Avis was telling us, like sponges taking in water. "I'm planning on going to North Carolina Central University in Durham. Y'all ought to go with me."

"Durham? I have an aunt that lives there. I might be able to stay with her," I said.

Avis became excited. "We could get an apartment and stay off campus together."

"Hey, wait. But I want to get married and have kids," I said.

"You can find a husband there. One with a college education." We all laughed self-consciously at the thought of going to college and finding a husband. One of the librarians looked our way. We looked at our books and turned pages. Avis said more quietly, "It helps you get into college if you do things like serve on student council in high school."

"Levonne, you should run for student council," Deborah suggested. "You like organizing things."

"Yeah." Beverly agreed.

Avis, Deborah and Beverly looked at me expectantly. I shrugged my shoulders upward and said, "I'll think about it." I felt excited and pleased that my friends believed in me enough to encourage me to exercise leadership skills. The confidence in myself that had been smashed over the previous two years at Star Elementary reconstituted itself a bit in that moment.

The thought of going to college and maybe finding my husband there was the most exciting thing that I had considered for my future. I liked the idea of living in a city where I had a relative. I decided that I would talk to Mrs. Richardson about it. She had lots of money. Maybe she would pay for my education.

28

Mrs. Richardson sipped chicken broth from a soup spoon. With my napkin in my lap, (as Mrs. Richardson had drilled into me to do since the day I arrived at her house two and a half years earlier) I dipped into my soup and rolled the spoon toward the back of the bowl instead of toward me, also as she had also taught.

I finished chewing the soft chicken and noodles, swallowed, and said as I looked at Mrs. Richardson, "I'm going to go to college."

"College? College? Now just how will you have that happen?" Mrs. Richardson sat her spoon down in the plate that held her bowl.

"You can get loans and grants and work study to pay for it." I sat my spoon down too.

"You know," Mrs. Richardson folded her napkin neatly. "Not everyone is suitable for college. Some people are made for other things." I listened quietly. "Some people are made for labor jobs." I must have looked perplexed. She explained, "The mills have to have people work in them."

Mrs. Richardson pushed her chair back. "There have to be people to take care of other people and their things."

"Yes. But you need to go to college if you want a good job."

"A good job? What do you know about a good job?" Mrs. Richardson rose from the table. "Your problem is that you want to live beyond your means."

Living beyond my means were new words for me. I wondered what significance the words held in my life. But I did not dare speak about it to Mrs. Richardson at that moment as she had become irritated. She was getting angry with me, it seemed. I thought of Teresa's mother, Mrs. Johnson, and all the other Brutonville teachers' faces flashed before me too. They had good jobs.

Mrs. Richardson walked her plate with bowl stacked on it in one hand and her china tea cup and saucer in the other to the sink. "Be careful with my cup. You know how easy they are to break."

"Yes ma'am," I responded, having heard for the one thousandth time about taking care of her china tea cups. It seemed that Mrs. Richardson believed that I was one of those people made not to go to college. I imagined ways I might *accidentally* crack her china cup.

29

I saw my brothers on the buses before and after school, but I did not talk with or see my parents for over four months by the winter of 1968. I was fourteen years old and a freshman in high school. At first, the months did not seem that long a time to be separated from my parents, but as the weeks stretched along, I missed them.

My life before, with my family, had necessitated that I master feelings of loneliness. When it struck, I knew to strike back with my thoughts. *I can withstand this. I can bare this feeling. I can get through this.* I learned to ride out the loneliness like a surfer riding a huge Hawaiian wave. I caught the wave of loneliness. I positioned myself over it. I let it flow along beneath me, beneath my surface, remaining untouched by its power and out of its grip.

Mama may have been knocked out from alcohol, Daddy might have been raging around like the Tasmanian devil, Lee lost in a book or watching Sunday football, Dale playing with his friends somewhere off in the neighborhood. It was a tricky balance with Frankie. He had always needed me to be the one he looked to, not the other way around. This in itself could be a salvation for me from loneliness or its trigger.

To remain free of loneliness' torture, I had to focus on the feeling, for if I lost focus, I could fall into it and my heart would ache not just for my current family situation, but for all the times in the past when I wanted to have and hold one of them but could not.

I knew that when I decided to reject a person or a situation, I had the ability to stick with my decision for a long time, regardless as to how much loneliness I felt. I did not easily forgive or forget. I was still angry with my father for yelling at me and shoving me during his wild rage.

∞

I began high school, my fourteenth birthday passed and Thanksgiving came and went without going to see my parents. But the truth is that they also did not come to see or call me either. This was the reality of my family, this family that I loved but could not for the life of me get their attention long enough to ever feel completely satisfied.

As Christmas break neared, I felt uncomfortable on my own. I dangled in the space between being someone's fourteen-year-old daughter and the unpaid live-in servant girl of an old woman. I reminded myself that I had made the decision to stay away from my father. The truth is that I did not have the power to get out of the position I was in. I thought that I had a lesson to teach my father about his raging and fighting, but for all I knew, he was oblivious to my gyrations. I had allowed myself to imagine that he might come running after me and apologize for his behavior.

During those nearly five months that I did not see my parents, Mrs. Richardson had become snappier and cooler toward me. I overheard her talking with her sister from Tennessee again. "She's so different. Now her mind is off thinking about boys and going to college."

Mrs. Richardson used every chance she could to reinforce her statements that all men are worthless. Each time that she said that it would be impossible for me to find a good man, I became more determined in my mind to have a husband one day.

When school recessed for the Christmas holidays, Mrs. Richardson's daughter, Macy, invited us to her house in Troy for dinner. I was excited because Macy and Harold's house was beautiful, and I loved visiting their daughter Candy's bedroom.

∞

Harold was the head executive officer of the local Coca Cola Bottling Company in Biscoe. Macy and Harold's house was a ranch style that sat on a hill north of Highway 20 between Troy and Biscoe. The winding driveway into their place passed over a brook and by stands of pines, oaks and maples. When I looked at their beautiful hill of trees, I could not help but recall the story of the black man that used to mow the grass and weeds off their property. His tractor flipped, trapped and killed him years earlier. As we approached the house, I thought of the man that I did not know, who died and left a wife and children behind.

The house was long and a beautiful gray, with rock walls

that reminded me of the Uwharrhie forest that it backed on to. The house looked to be a part of the natural landscape.

Mrs. Richardson and I never entered Macy's house through the front door. We entered through the large garage into a hallway with a washer and dryer and a room that Mrs. Richardson said was for their maid. We traveled from the laundry room and maid's quarters into the kitchen and den area. The den had windows from ceiling to floor that looked onto the backyard. There was a large fireplace in the den and a television.

The kitchen was bright from light coming through windows that looked out to the winding driveway. The kitchen sparkled. Glass and metal surfaces glistened throughout.

Harold nodded his head and said "Hello" in a way that made me feel insignificant. Maybe it was that he did not look at me, but past me when he spoke.

Macy popped lime green daiquiris into the freezer for the night's desert. "Hi Levonne. How was high school this year?"

"Good, thank you."

"Did you pass all your classes?"

"Yes ma'am."

I enjoyed watching Macy concentrate on the fixings for the meal to come. "We're having steak, asparagus and baked potato for dinner, Mother. Do you want your steak medium or well?"

Meals at Macy and Harold's were always the same and always delicious. I had had my first steak, asparagus and baked potato there.

While dinner was being prepared, I was allowed to go back into Candy's room. Candy went to Meredith College, a school for young women in Raleigh. Though home from college for the holidays, she had already left on a date for the evening. Candy had the most gorgeous long blond hair and a beautiful face. She had always been friendly toward me and taught me, by my listening to her on the telephone, how to act very excited about something (no matter how you might really feel) when you talked with your friends.

Next to watching Candy get herself ready for a date, I loved listening to records on her record player. My favorite thing was to listen to *The Sound of Music* album.

Julie Andrews sang "Edelweiss, Going on Seventeen, How do You Solve a Problem Like Maria." I learned most of the words for the songs from all the times that I spent in Candy's room.

For dinner, as usual, Macy placed my plate of delicious food atop a bamboo place mat on a wooden TV tray in the den. I watched television while Mrs. Richardson, Macy and Harold ate in their formal dining room that looked down the hill to the front of their property.

Since I knew very well how to be by myself, I ate my food and enjoyed every single bite of it while I listened to Cronkite and Reasoner talk about the U.S. POW's released from Viet Cong prisons and the Hong Kong flu pandemic that was sweeping the country. Though it felt natural to be on my own, I found it harder and harder to ride the wave of loneliness for my own family that continued to intrude itself into my reality.

30

Mrs. Richardson's phone did not ring often. When it did, it was usually one of her children. Two days before Christmas in the middle of the morning, while I used an old toothbrush to apply polish in the crevices of Mrs. Richardson's silver tea pot set, the phone rang.

"Hello. Iola Richardson's residence... Yes... Hello Ovella." I stopped brushing the silver when I heard my mother's name. Mrs. Richardson turned from the dining room buffet cabinet where the phone sat and looked into the kitchen at me. Something was wrong. Mama did not use Mr. Boyd's telephone casually. "What do you say happened? Uh huh... Uh huh... Yes. Yes. You want me to bring Levonne home?" She looked down at the floor, then turned back around and faced away from me. "When did you want her there?... Now?... Alright then. We'll see you in ten minutes."

"What is it?" I asked Mrs. Richardson immediately upon her return of the phone to its cradle.

"Your father is sick. Paramedics are working on him. She wants you there." She turned toward her bedroom. "I don't know what usefulness having you there is going to make in the situation." Her voice trailed off, before she lifted her voice back toward me again, "Get ready."

I took off the cotton gloves and the apron as I wondered what was wrong with Daddy. I took a heavy sweater from my closet, then joined Mrs. Richardson in the Saratoga. We drove the majority of the five minutes in silence. With my concern over my father's safety, I felt my love for him swell. I had kept all my feelings for him except anger under wraps for months. During those few minutes of the drive, my resolve over the previous months not to see him so as to teach him a lesson about his raging was gone.

As we approached my parents' house, Mrs. Richardson said, "You can't go in. He may have that Hong Kong flu. If I get it, it will kill me."

We sat in the car in my mother's gravel and red-soil drive-way about fifty feet from my parent's front door steps. Mrs. Richardson tooted the horn. My mother came and walked to the car. Through the car window that had been rolled down about five inches, the two women spoke.

"What's the matter with him?"

Mama stooped a bit and looked over at me. She tightened her thin jacket around her as the wind gusted. "He was out slaughtering a hog and the next thing you knew he came in the house and said he felt funny. Then he fell out cold on the living room floor." I leaned in so that I could see my mother's face. I looked toward the house and saw Lee and Dale through the front door's window pane as they passed from one room to the next. "I called the ambulance and they came out. But by then he had come to. They wanted to take him to the hospital, but Rob said he didn't need to go. So they left him here."

"What's wrong with him?" Mrs. Richardson insisted. Frankie emerged from the house, ran down the steps and was standing by my side of the car as Mama continued in the conversation with Mrs. Richardson. He put his hand on the car's door handle and I shook my head at him.

Mama said, "We don't know what's wrong. The paramedics couldn't say. That's why they wanted him to go to the hospital."

"It might be the Hong Kong flu," Mrs. Richardson insisted. I looked at my brother standing beside the car, waiting for me to get out. "So I don't want Levonne to go inside. If I get it, it will kill me. Your husband is young and strong. He can fight off whatever it is."

I looked from Frankie to Mama. Mama searched my face for *my* desire in the situation. I did not want to be responsible for killing Mrs. Richardson with the Hong Kong flu, and since my father was better, and though I had not seen him for nearly five months and although it was only two days from Christmas, I decided that I could see him some other time. I was silent. I sat back in my seat and allowed Mrs. Richardson to have the control over my life. "Alright then," Mama said. "We'll see you later. Hope y'all have a good Christmas." Mama sounded her usual hospitable self.

∞

Christmas had always been my most favorite time of the year. In years past, I had loved gathering a cedar tree from the woods with my father and decorating it with Mama.

251

Using the ornaments that we had used for my entire life in my family–pink and blue and orange metallic bulbs that we always managed to break several of each Christmas season, the two strings of lights that we wrapped around the tree from top to bottom, and the silvery icicles, that we needed a new pack or two of each year.

I had loved Christmas days of the past with my brothers. Bags of hard candies. Baskets of oranges and apples and pecans and walnuts, none of which we ever saw the quantity and variety of in our house at any other time of year. My parents watched us as we fondled and fawned over whatever it was we had been given, them expressing the kind of joy that parents experience from seeing their children's happiness.

Sitting there in Mrs. Richardson's car, I did not remind myself, as I ached for Christmas with my family, that before any Christmas Day in the past was over, all hell would have broken lose because both my parents would have celebrated all day until my father's raging was in full force. No matter, I acquiesced to protect Mrs. Richardson from the flu that frightened her enough to keep a girl away from a sick father at Christmas time.

31

On Christmas day of 1968, a second call came to Mrs. Richardson's house from my mother to summon me back to the home of my parents and three brothers.

"He must have the Hong Kong flu," Mrs. Richardson insisted as we drove the five miles to my mother's house. "You cannot go in. I don't know what good she thinks you being there is going to do. They've called the ambulance." I listened as Mrs. Richardson rattled on about what might be wrong with my father, and what I was not going to do. "If I am exposed to the flu, it will kill me." I wondered how old Mrs. Richardson was. People from Dunn-Green Town speculated that she was in her seventies, if not her eighties. She would not tell her age. I had asked.

I was quiet. I did not want Mrs. Richardson to die. But I also wanted to see my father. This was the second call from my mother, saying that my father had fainted and become unresponsive, over the span of three days. Mama wanted me home. I had not seen my father in nearly five months. I didn't know what good Mama thought I would be there with them, but she had called and I was determined that I was going to see my father this time.

We drove into my mother's yard. In front of the house sat a white ambulance truck with red lettering on it. As soon as Mrs. Richardson came to a halt, and before she turned off the engine, I exited the car. "Wait Levonne. Don't go in there."

I went inside the house that stood with the door half ajar, though the temperature was too cool to have the door left open. Inside was my mother stood back from the paramedics who were taking my father's blood pressure. "His heart is fine. His pulse is low. His blood pressure is low," the younger paramedic spoke calmly to the older one. My seven-year-old brother Frankie came to my side.

A Christmas tree that seemed smaller than ones I recalled from our past and less decorated than I recalled sat in a corner. The smell of cedar, burning wood smoke and cigarette smoke permeated the air.

"He's not responding. Mr. Gaddy. Mr Gaddy. Can you hear me?" Both paramedics looked at my father. "His respiration is shallow. Let's take him in."

"We're taking him to the hospital," the older paramedic said to my mother.

"Okay." She looked at me.

"I want to go too, Mama." I said.

Lee and Dale rushed into the house. "What's wrong?" Lee asked.

Mama explained that Daddy had come in the house from outside, saying that he felt dizzy again. He sat down and then fell out on the couch and had not reawakened.

"Me and Levonne are going in the ambulance to the hospital," Mama told Lee.

∞

Outside, Mrs. Richardson, seeing that I had made my choice, left me to be with my family on that Christmas Day.

∞

My mother and I were silent on the fifteen minute ride from Dunn-Green Town in Star to the hospital in Troy. My father lay there on the gurney not speaking, not opening his eyes. I touched his hand. It was rough. It was large. But it was also soft in places. *My father's face looks pained,* I thought, *like he is having a bad dream.* My mother had a worried look on her face as she and I held onto our seats through the swerves of Okeeweemee Road. The road that I had ridden with parents and neighbors from Dunn-Green Town through the Uwharrie forest many times before. I remembered how much fun the ride had been when there was not a sick person on board being rushed to the hospital in an ambulance with a groaning siren.

"Your father hated that job at the mill." Mama talked as the ambulance approached the hospital driveway. I had learned about the most recent change in job from Lee months earlier. "He liked working outside." Mama seemed contemplative as she spoke. "When he left J.P.'s sawmill, there wasn't another job anywhere around here for him. J.P. said it was too dangerous for your daddy working on them saws and things." I did not know much about what had caused the "new" danger in a job that my father had done for years. But *of course,* I thought, *it had to be the alcohol.*

32

My mother and I spent two nights in Durham with my father's sister, Aunt Janie, waiting for my father to wake from his coma, which he did not do. The hospital staff had not been able to help him in Troy.

When we returned back home to Star, Mama gave reports to my brothers and the neighbors about my father's health condition. "He's not looking too good. He's in a coma. The doctors don't know if he is going to make it."

"You don't say," Mr. Boyd said as Mama laid it all out before him.

"The doctor said he had never seen a sinus infection so bad. He said that he drained gallons of mucous from Rob's sinuses. He wondered how Rob lived with the pain it must have caused."

"For Lord's sake. I'll say a prayer for him, Misrus Gaddy."

"I sure do thank you, Mr. Boyd. We'll get that rent paid just as soon as we can."

"Don't worry yourself just now. You take care of your childrens."

"I thank you."

After Mr. Boyd left our house, I asked my mother what

she was planning to do for money. I had not given the finances of our family much thought until that moment of needing to pay twelve dollars of house rent and not having it.

I had not appreciated how much our family had depended on my father's income. His earnings paid the rent, bought the groceries, my family's clothing and the old car acquired recently that did not run half the time since Daddy started his job at the hosiery mill.

"Your father hated that job. His sinuses were horrible from smelling that dye all night long," Mama paused. "I'm going to have to get some money from somewhere, because we are going to need to eat."

"Can you get a job Mama?" I asked.

"I've been thinking about that. I've been wishing I had gone to school to be a nurse like I wanted to when I was a young woman."

"You wanted to be a nurse?"

"Yes I've always wanted to be a nurse."

"You never told us that before."

"Well there hasn't been any need to talk about it."

"Why didn't you go, Mama?"

"Cause I married and had you children."

"I want to go to college when I finish high school." I looked at Mama's face.

"That's good. But you know I can't help you. We don't have any money for college."

"I can get loans and grants and do work study."

"You can get all that?" I nodded my head. "You should do

it then. You'll be glad of it for you whole life. Children are supposed to do better in their lives than their parents were able to do."

∞

The night that we returned from Durham to my mother's house in Star, I lowered myself onto my knees. I felt the rough surface of the scuffed vinyl rug as I leaned against the squeaky couch in the part of the living room that had become my bedroom. With absolute earnestness and faith, I focused my fourteen-year-old mind and prayed.

There was no curtain between my room and the adjoining den where my mother and brothers watched television. No curtain allowed my mother to witness my earnestness. Somehow I believed this witnessing gave more strength to my prayer.

Dear God is how I started my appeal to our most powerful Lord during my period of greatest need. *Dear God, please return my father home from the hospital. I know that he has not always been the best man. He has beaten my mother and he drinks and cusses. But my family needs him. My mother cannot take care of us by herself. She does not have a job and does not know how she will pay for rent and food. Since I know that you are fair, that you are merciful and that you love my family, I know that you will return our father, because without him we cannot live. Dear God, please also take care of my brothers and my mother. I know I can depend on you. Amen.*

I arose from my knees and slipped beneath the sheet and blankets, tuned the radio by my head to the soul station out of Charlotte, moved my mind to dreams of college, of love,

259

of marriage, of my own family one day, and tried not to feel afraid. I felt my family's fragileness all around me.

∞

Since Daddy did not have the Hong Kong flu but had a non-contagious form of meningitis instead, Mrs. Richardson allowed me back. I explained to her what was happening with my family.

"Daddy is in intensive care at Durham Memorial Hospital. He is on machines that are keeping him breathing. He has tubes going in and out of his body."

"It sounds serious."

"Yes, the doctor wondered if he had a brain tumor. He wondered if Daddy had been aggressive."

"I see."

"I know that he is going to get better. I am certain of it. Mama and my brothers need our father to take care of them. Mama is wondering where she is going to get money for the rent and for food."

"Oh! Your mother is a wasteful woman. She has thrown more out the back door than your father could bring in the front door."

Mrs. Richardson's words slapped me in my face. What did she mean that my mother was wasteful? What gave her the right to say such a thing? The only thing I saw my mother throw out the back door was dirty dish water. Mrs. Richardson's words sounded mean to me. The words caught me off guard. I stored them away for further examination.

I continued the ritual of prayer once I returned to Mrs.

Richardson's and after I went back to school from Christmas break.

Ms. McDuffie, my English teacher, talked about the old woman named Mrs. Havasham and a girl named Estella that lived with her in the Charles Dickens story *Great Expectations*. I was involved in the story when on that winter January morning in 1969, one month after my daddy went into the hospital, the intercom came on telling Ms. McDuffie to send Levonne Gaddy to the office.

The next thing I knew was that Lee and I were in the backseat of the principal's fresh, clean smelling car. I did not notice Joe Britt's fruit and vegetable stand that my mother, brothers and I had walked to when I was young, or Star Elementary where I had spent two years of my school life, or even Mrs. Richardson's.

I recalled a recent conversation between my mother and me. I had ridden my bicycle to her house in the cold. She reported that Daddy was hooked to yet more machines and that he was still in a coma in intensive care.

"It doesn't look good," she said.

"You have to believe in his will to live Mama. You have to believe that he is going to live." I almost pleaded with her as she continued on her report.

"The doctors are saying he might not make it."

"Our belief is what will save Daddy." I had felt angry that my mother seemed disconnected from her husband, resigned to his demise. He was just a man in the hospital, near death to her. *Where is her faith in God?* I had asked myself.

My mother's absence from my world of absolute faith meant that I had had to pray even harder, that I had had to believe not just for me, but for her also. I did my best with faith and prayer and I did an excellent job of it. So when I was summoned from my ninth grade English class to the principal's office, I was beyond disappointment with God for rejecting my prayers.

On that car ride from high school to my mother's house, I wondered where the *merciful God* was. *How could God take away a man with an unemployed wife and three children for whom to care?* I was also sure that because my father was not *saved* in the church and because of his sinning, he was bound to go to hell. I wondered how a merciful God could take Daddy away and on top of that say that I would never get to see him again, even in heaven. I wondered what good my faith and prayers had been.

33

Oh how I had wanted a chance to talk with my father before he died. I spent five months rejecting him. Our last interaction was bad. He yelled at me and shoved me. I swore I would stand up for myself, that I would not allow him to abuse me as he had my mother. I stayed away from him to teach him a lesson. I had wanted to talk with him in the ambulance on the way to the hospital, but he was already in a coma. He did not witness nor hear about my prayers for him during the last month as he lay in the hospital with tubes and machines holding him to life.

∞

A long black wool coat hung on the back of my parents' bedroom door. The last time my father had worn the coat must have been when they courted, before I or my three brothers were born. The coat, I am sure, represented, at the time of wearing it, sophistication, style, romance. It was a nice coat.

Daddy wore blue denim overalls and a white t-shirt year round, with Brogan work boots. The black coat had hung from the backs of bedroom doors in several houses, collecting dust on its shoulders. I imagined Daddy in his coat with a dark Stetson hat. I imagined him dressed in a white shirt and tie. I imagined him smiling through an alcohol-infected mood at my mother. The two of them laughing together.

That would have been before they married. That would have been when he picked her up on her day off from her live–in nanny job. That would have been on their drives from Randolph County down Highway I-40 to Montgomery County. During that time when Daddy courted Mama and wore his long black coat, they had no idea what was ahead for them. What would they have done if they had known that they would drink enough alcohol between them to fill a small pond? That he would beat on her for over a decade and that she would passively participate in it for as long? That one of their children would get his brain pickled by the alcohol going through my mother's uterus before even being born? And that Daddy would die at fifty-six, leaving a jobless thirty-something-year-old wife to raise four children alone? What would they have done if they had known all that?

34

During those days after my father died, in the winter of my fourteenth year, I hated everything and everyone. My mother became a syrupy excuse of a survivor, talking at me as though she understood and cared about what I must be going through.

The weather was cold. Thirty-five degrees fahrenheit. Leaves hardened and fell from trees after a death that had sucked every bit of color and subtleness from them. Grass turned the color of straw. Fields grayed into stiletto stick masses. The ground softened from rain then froze again. I hated the cold, the wetness, the mud, the bare trees. I hated winter and my mother more than I had ever hated anything before.

According to the doctor that one and only time my mother and I visited Daddy in the hospital during his last thirty days of life on earth, tons of mucous had been drained out of his sinuses, and they wondered if he had a brain tumor, in addition to the meningitis. The doctor asked "Is he aggressive? The tumor is in a location that would have made him aggressive." My mother does not answer but stares off into space. I feel embarrassment and look away from the doctor when his eyes turn to me.

For the remainder of the thirty days, my father lay in that Durham hospital bed with machines swooshing air into his body and bottles dripping liquids into his veins and with nobody from our house to say to him, "You can make it Rob." *What was wrong with Mama that she did not go back to see him? What wife leaves a man in a coma to look out for himself?* These were my thoughts.

∞

"Get your coat on. It's time to go to the funeral home." Mama spoke in that mother-love tone that did not fit her. "Let's go." She stood with the door open. A cold draft wafted in and whipped around me like a lasso and dragged me out of the house. The cold and the wetness on the winter day of that new year made the year feel old.

My feet took me down the three damp concrete steps, along the rocky driveway and into the back seat of my neighbor's faded green station wagon. What can you do when you hate something so, and when you are as sick of a thing as you could ever be of anything, and when you are just one instance away from exploding from all the anger you feel inside? What can you do when you are fourteen and you have prayed to God for weeks for your father's life and your prayers have been shunned? What do you do when your father who was nothing close to perfect, but who was the one who provided for a wife and children is taken away? I knew I had to keep my distance from the whole matter of my daddy's death or a poisonous trouble that nobody could imagine might explode from me.

When we passed Mrs. Richardson's house, I felt hate for her. It was her fault that I had not seen my father while he was able to talk with me, during the period preceding his month-long hospitalization. If she had let me see my father the first time I was called to him rather than making me sit in her car in front of my parents' house, protecting her from exposure to what she feared was the Hong Kong flu, I would have spoken to him one last time. "It will kill me if I get it," she had said. My fourteen-year-old brain could not resolve the selfishness of her drive to survive against my need to have talked with my father before he died.

I reviewed in my mind multiple times how Mama had left me in Mrs. Richardson's car and did not insist that I go in to see him. It was her fault, too, that he and I had not had a chance to forgive one another face to face. She left me there in the front seat of the turquoise and white Saratoga with the windows closed and the information that Daddy had pulled through his fainting spell. Those moments were the last opportunity I had to see my father conscious and aware of who I was to him.

∞

I trailed behind Mama as she walked toward my father's casket. I watched her as she went to him and touched his hands that lay folded over his gray-jacketed solar plexus. His hands were ashy, not the rich brown that I had known. My mother touched his face. It was gray too. She looked at me. "Come on," she reached out her hand to me to draw me closer. I took one step forward, aware that the hand that reached for me was the hand that had just touched the dead man in the casket. I did not want her hand on me. I stood beside her as she rubbed on the body that my father had lived in for the fourteen years of my life.

"He's cold," she said as she leaned over him. "You can touch him." I did not move. As she motioned for me with her eyes and that hand of hers again, I felt a rage rise in me. I could not take it any longer. Some of the words that I had practiced with Ola Mae years before puked out of me.

"Fuck this shit!" My mother's eyes grew large as I turned and blindly ran out of the funeral home. I had walked the four miles between downtown Star where Phillips Funeral Home stood to the black neighborhood many times. On that day in the winter cold and wetness, I ran the entire way back home as fast as I could, stopping only to toss rocks at Mrs. Richardson's house.

I took shelter under the trees on the north side of my parents' house. There, I huddled beneath the leafless limbs and between the gray-barked tree trunks until my body's sweat turned me cold. But I did not cry. I refused to believe that my father was truly gone from earth. A child can think incredible things when she is terrified of what is in store for her future.

35

Soggy shoes are wiped and scraped on steps before coming inside our house to stand near a toasty woodstove. Hundred watt bulbs hang from the sockets in the living room ceiling. A yellow white glow lights every corner, every face, and every picture on the wall—photographs of Grandma Idella, Uncle Will, and a glossy cardboard print of Jesus Christ at the last supper.

One bulb lights the record player that sits quiet with the Jackson Five albums stacked vertically beneath it. The sofa without arms and the bedspread that covers it will soon have many bottoms on it. Afterwards it will serve as my bed. My father and mother's siblings will arrive at different times. The neighbors who are already with us act happy. They say to one another, "This is not the time to drink. Let's respect the dead tonight."

I linger in my parents' bedroom, away from the living room that is filling with people paying respect with food and soft laughter and comments of comfort for my mother. "You gonna get through this Ovella. The Lord is with you. I'll pray for you and the children. Lord bless you, Child."

I look around the bedroom. A fifty watt bulb hangs from

the ceiling socket. Clothes on hooks adorn all but one wall. Their bed slumps in the middle. A smooth cotton bedspread covers it and two flat pillows that they have had since forever lay at the top end of the bed. *Pillows are not a priority in my family* I think.

A big dresser crowds the end of the bed. A wardrobe and a bureau cabinet leave just enough room for one person to take a bath from an aluminum pan or to dress or undress. Daddy's stuff is everywhere. The long black wool coat. A black suit in the wardrobe. T-shirts, socks and boxer shorts lay in the second drawer of the dresser. The missing top drawer allows me to peer in at Daddy's things. I reach in to feel for horehound candy. There is not any.

Important papers fill the drawers of the bureau cabinet—old driver's licenses, metal social security cards. Magazines with pictures of actresses that I have never heard of or seen. A few black and whites of naked women that my parents did not know us children knew about. Boxes of pictures sit on the bureau shelf above the mirror, filled with images of relatives' lives. I glance at myself in the mirror. I am doing a good job of not showing what is inside. I check the pleasant look that I carry for others, then allow my face to return to the expressionless place.

The smell of rain on earth wafts in through the slightly-opened window and mixes with what seems in my mind to be the lingering smells of Daddy's sweaty work clothes. I again put my hand through the opening left by the absent drawer and feel Daddy's clothing. Worn, soft cotton. I let my hand rest there; then allow the fabric to caress it as I draw my hand slowly away. I feel an ache in my gut. The quiet and calm in the room without my father is an incredible contrast to the Tasmanian devil kind of energy that he exuded when alive. I miss his presence but allow myself to soak in the new peacefulness.

I open the door to leave the bedroom. The bright yellow-white light from the living room's bulb fills my eyes and seems to almost hurt my skin as I enter. Simultaneously, I become concerned that the light makes me look whiter than I am. I shrink a bit and wish I had clothes on that covered every part of me instead of the short-sleeved dress that I had chosen to wear for my father's wake.

The people sitting in our living room see me, but they don't notice that I am more than the daughter of the man that had lived there. They don't know that I am a whole other person, not just a neighbor or a niece, or a daughter, or a sister or a friend, but was also a refugee from my family. I take the people in through my eyes. I wonder how much of who I am and who I am not they can see. I am ashamed for the daughter that I was.

Then I see him. Fred, the distant cousin. The one who broke my private parts. He is smiling. I count the eleven slow steps to him past Bernice, who checks my face, then looks where I am looking, at Fred, and then back to me. All the other neighbors don't miss a beat in talking with one another.

"How you doing?" He reaches past another boy that came with him to our house at the same time as Aunt Annie comes through the door with a big smile. "Hey, Pumpkin.

271

How're you?" She squeezes me. Then he touches me. He puts his arm around my shoulders and pulls me against his side. My body becomes stone. I smile. It is my daddy's wake. These people are our company. I say *hey* to his friend.

I avoid Fred's eyes. When I think that I have stood next to him long enough, I break away and talk with my Aunt.

She has come prepared to pierce my ears for me. That night. Right there. I fetch ice cubes from the tray in our refrigerator freezer and after she has held them on my ear-lobes long enough, she makes holes with a needle that she has sterilized by heating with a cigarette lighter. I am uncomfortable having Fred watch me as my aunt struggles to push the needle further beneath the skin. Further into the hole she is creating in my earlobe. My head moves as she tugs. "Stay still now," she says. A pinch is all I feel through the numbness. "You're tough," she says to me as she wrestles through the skin and the cartilage.

"It doesn't hurt," I tell her and look at Fred when I say the words, though he is not listening and has begun talking with other relatives that have arrived. I want those gold studs that Aunt Annie brought for me to wear for weeks until the holes in my earlobes have healed.

I am pleased when Fred and his friend leave. Afterward, I don't give him a second thought. I talk with my neighbors and my other relatives and I feel their presence. They are people who are planted solid with strong bodies and minds and spirits. They are precious and they hold me with their eyes and their voices. "Come here, Girl, and sit down beside me." Bernice pulls me down onto the couch, making room for me to squeeze in. She pulls me close to her. I let myself be there, to be with these people. For a while, I feel whole and perfect.

36

After my father's funeral, Mama made plans to have a neighbor take her to the Social Security Administration office in Troy to apply for survivor's benefits so she could take care of our family. She also planned to begin a nursing program at Montgomery Technical Institute.

"If my daughter can go to college, I guess I can go to the technical institute and study nursing," Mama said.

As the time approached for me to go back to Mrs. Richardson's and back to school, I was not ready. I wanted to stay with Frankie, Lee, Dale and my mother, even if I was still mad with her. The idea of driving around the country with Mrs. Richardson in her Saratoga had held appeal. But for the first time, the price to remain in her home under her direction, just so I could take a drive to another state, felt too high.

Simultaneously, Mrs. Richardson and Mama set in motion their plan for me to return to my job. In Mrs. Richardson's car, while riding back to her house, I reflected on the words she had told me less than two months earlier. "There are no good men left in the world. Boys are like dogs chasing after a bitch in heat." She did not want, nor believe, that I should think that there was a viable future for me with a male. Her picture of us, in my mind, as travel companions had taken the shape of an unnatural future for a young girl to consider. I looked at the elderly woman beside me driving the large car and thought *This is not right.*

Back at Mrs. Richardson's, the first thing that I found the nerve to tell her was what had been on my mind about her actions.

"Are your clothes ready for school Monday? Do you need to do a load of laundry?"

"Yes, ma'am. I need clean clothes."

"I have a basket full too."

I felt edgy with Mrs. Richardson. Her home felt foreign to me. I felt the way you feel when you know you don't want to be in a place, but you think you have to be there. Without my father alive, she seemed somehow extra.

"Mrs. Richardson." The woman stopped writing on the shopping list that she was making and focused on me. "The last time that my daddy was conscious was that first time Mama called to have me go home and see him."

"Yes." Mrs. Richardson wrote down another thing to buy for her canasta card luncheon.

"Well, he was unconscious after that day, and I didn't get to talk with him again before he died." Mrs. Richardson looked at me with questioning eyes. "I didn't get to talk with him anymore. My last chance was that day. You wouldn't let me go in."

"You hadn't been home for months before that, if I recall."

"Yes but I was there on that day."

"So what are you saying?"

"That that was the last time I could have talked with him."

"Is there something you think I should do about that?"

"No. Not now. But..."

Mrs. Richardson gazed at me with her gray eyes. "Hurry up now. We don't have all day for that laundry. I need you to run to the store for these things."

In that moment, with that interchange, I realized that I would never be her family. I would always just be her help. We stared at one another.

"You'll understand one day. When *you're* old."

As I gathered my dirty things and Mrs. Richardson's basket of clothing and headed for the basement, I felt haunted by heavy thoughts. *Was it Mrs. Richardson's fault that my daddy died not knowing I was finished being mad at him? Or mine?* My mind seemed to be speeding back and forth attempting to determine whose fault it was that I had not reconnected with him.

∞

While checking the settings on the washing machine, I reminded myself of Mrs. Richardson's directive that I should not ever mix her clothes with mine. After loading the tub with my things, I tossed two dish towels, her face cloth, the sweater that she put over her shoulders at night, and all her underwear into the metal receptacle, right along with my clothes. I smiled and in my mind invited her to come down and find the evidence of my disobedience.

From behind the *National Geographics*, I pulled the box of letters that I had been writing to Reubin Martinez. I unfolded blank paper and retrieved the ink pen from the box and began to write.

—

Dear Reuben,

I hope that you are doing alright in Vietnam, or if you're lucky, in Korea. I hope that it will not be long before you are back home in the San Fernando Valley with your family. I know you must miss them. I'm realizing that family is very important.

My daddy died. I have just spent a lot of time with my mother and brothers and I have to tell you that for the first time in a long time, I liked being around them. I have lots of uncles and aunts, same as you. They all love me.

Mostly right now, I look forward to finishing high school and being on my own. I'm going to college in Durham with a girlfriend of mine. I am still planning to come out to see you in California when I am on my own and when you are back home with your family.

I'm going to go now, Reuben. There is laundry to put in the dryer and another load to wash. And I have a trip to the grocery store to make. Take care of yourself.

Yours Truly, Levonne

—

I folded the letter and instead of stashing the box behind the magazines so that Mrs. Richardson would not discover it, I put the box of letters in the laundry basket.

I climbed the concrete steps to the backyard garden area.

I then climbed the wooden stairs to my room's door. After dropping the laundry basket with the letter box in it on the floor, I walked into the dining room where Mrs. Richardson was taking cloth napkins out of a buffet drawer and laying them on the dining room table. "What took so long? The store closes in less than an hour."

"Mrs. Richardson." I stood tall in front of the woman.

"Yes?" She continued examining each napkin.

"Mrs. Richardson," I said more firmly. She looked at me from her task. "You said that college is beyond my means, but I *am* going to college. I am going to get a good job one day and take care of myself." She stood quietly listening. "And Mrs. Richardson, I don't want to stay here anymore. I want to go back and live with my family."

"What? Why would you want to do that? You don't even have a place to sleep down there."

"There's enough space. I want to be with my family."

"Your mother doesn't want you there. She's told me so."

"She has?"

"Yes, she knows that you want to chase boys." I felt a shot of nausea in my stomach. "Your mother has said that she is glad you have a place to stay, because there is not room for you there."

"I'm going home Mrs. Richardson," I said knowing that I would and could deal with Mama soon enough. "You've already kept me from daddy's last day of consciousness and I'm not going to let you keep me from the rest of my family. If you don't want to drive me home, I can take my bicycle." I turned toward my room.

"Oh no, you aren't going to take that bicycle. Those boys will have that torn up before a day has passed. No. No. That stays here." In my room, I took from the closet my mother's old suitcase that I had used to transport my things a dozen times the past two and a half years. From my bedroom doorway, the older woman asked with disbelief in her voice, "So you're serious?"

As Mrs. Richardson examined my actions with her eyes, I stood tall again. "Mrs. Richardson, I'm going to get married one day to someone who is as good as your Foster was." To those words she was silent.

I used brown paper bags for my things that did not fit into the suitcase. As I packed, I thought, *It's alright if my family is used to having me gone. I am used to being gone. We will just both have to get used to one other again.*

Mrs. Richardson drove me home. When I lugged my things from the car, my mother, having stepped outside to greet us, asked, "Levonne, what are you doing?"

"I'm coming back home to stay."

Mama looked at Mrs. Richardson who, from her seated position at the wheel of her car said, "I told her you didn't have room down here for her, but she insisted." By then, Lee and Dale's attention had shifted from the football players falling around in the snow and mud on television and peered out of the window to see what we were up to outside.

"Well," Mama said. "These are tight quarters." She then folded her arms and rubbed them with her hands.

Frankie busted out of the house as I approached the steps. "Carry this," I handed him a bag and brushed past Mama.

Once inside, Lee and Dale's attention returned to the televised ball game while I retrieved the last of my possessions. Mrs. Richardson said some final things to my mother and left.

∞

Although my mother, at first, put forth a front of it being a bad idea for me to return home, I knew that her words were like melting margarine. There would be no resistance to the natural forces of my growing up. She was too distracted by her own needs, and she needed me to help her as much as I needed to be in their world.

Mrs. Richardson's place and things became memories. The bedroom where I slept, the clean top and bottom sheets, an inside bathroom, the fresh smelling shower, my own towel, the tidy kitchen counter with the toaster, cake mixer, and automatic can opener, the *National Geographics*, the basement with the automatic washer and dryer, and my blue bicycle. I left those things behind and remade my life with my brothers and mother in Dunn-Green Town while I dreamed of going to college and finding a husband one day.

37

"Mama. That's pretty." I looked at the picture on the Butterick pattern envelope. We had picked out the material for my high school graduation clothes the weekend before. Solid red polyester for the pants and a red and white jersey print material for the wrap-around top. I pictured myself wearing the outfit beneath the black graduation gown and later in college.

"This material is easy to work with." Mama guided the jersey under the needle of the Elna sewing machine that her boyfriend had given to her.

"I'm gonna buy clothes with the hundred dollars Lee sent me." I pressed the five twenty dollar bills to my chest. I felt wealthy. The new clothes, Lee's gift in my hands and college just a few months away.

"You better save that for your school books. Remember the letter said you would need to buy your books."

"How far is Fort Bragg?"

"Just a few hours." Mama looked at me from her sewing.

"I guess he'll be jumping out of airplanes when I go to get my diploma." I pictured Lee in his military uniform as he stood in formation with his 82nd Airborne battalion. I reflected on his generosity. Whenever he had something, he had shared it with us, his siblings; even if it meant that he did not have that much left over for himself.

"Here, try this top on. Let's check the hemline." I pulled the material on over my tank top. I wrapped the slinky blouse around me and tied the belt. It felt cool against my skin.

My mind was already gone from my mother's house. I was already in Durham and beyond. "Mama, I'm gonna travel. I can't wait to go to California after college and visit with Reuben Martinez and his family. Remember him?"

"You don't know where that boy is now."

"Yes, but I told him that I would see him in California one day, so I'm going to find him!"

While Mama pinned the sleeves with straight pins, I imagined beaches and sand and palm trees. I imagined Reuben's big Puerto Rican family buzzing around each other at a big family picnic. I had lost touch with the young soldier that I'd met four years earlier, but I still had the California address he'd given me. *I WILL find them* I thought.

"Mama. I think I want to be a flight attendant so that I can fly around the country, around the world."

"How you gonna do all those things? Take that off."

Mama stood back and watched me remove the blouse, then went to the ironing board and began pressing the hem into the sleeves. The steam rose from the iron and dissipated instantly into the humid May air. Mama took the blouse back to her chair and began sewing the hem into the sleeves.

Frankie came into the house, running as usual. He was ten. He was finishing the fourth grade at Star Elementary. "Heyyyyy." He strung the word out for as long as he could and laughed as he watched us watching him frolic.

"What do you think you're doing?" Mama asked. He just laughed. We all three laughed.

Mama in a very deliberate manner put down her sewing. She stood. "Okay. I was going to wait 'til your graduation day, but you need your present now. Come on." She grabbed the car keys and motioned for me to follow her as she walked toward the front door. Frankie joined in the procession to her boyfriend's car. A blue Chevrolet that Mama borrowed whenever she needed to drive back and forth from Star to his house in Troy.

I wondered if we were going somewhere and could not imagine what I would be getting that would necessitate us driving. I hugged Frankie around the shoulders and was surprised when Mama went to the trunk of the car, rather than getting into the driver's seat.

"What is it?" I could barely contain myself. Mama popped the trunk open with a click as she turned the key. I looked in. "What is it?" I said, as I peered inside to a trunk full of red. There were suitcases in the trunk. Red suitcases. Three of them. "Wow!" I looked at Frankie and shook his shoulders. He laughed his joyful laugh.

I looked at Mama. "Well, go ahead. Take them out."

The handles of the three suitcases were black. I took the largest out. Its emptiness felt light. I removed the medium sized one and gave it to Frankie to carry, and grabbed the overnight case with my empty hand. I stood with the two suitcases dangling at the ends of my arms and with a heart-felt smile thanked my mother.

She smiled back. "You're welcome. I thought you'd need them with all the traveling you're planning to do." Mama looked away from me, her face taking on a more sober look and closed the trunk. All I could think was how happy I was that my dream of leaving home and going to college was coming true.

∞

The last summer with my family was a splendid blue one. Everything had meaning and I practiced as best I could, the launched-young-adult identity that had been my reality since my high school graduation on May 30, 1972.

That summer, the PACE program employed me and several boys from my neighborhood. I worked as a secretary in the sleepy main office at Star Elementary. Most of the time, I was the only one there as the principal was out making trips to this place and that around the county. The work experience of me being mostly on my own bred no loneliness.

38

On the first Sunday in September of 1972, just three weeks before my eighteenth birthday, Mama in a pretty blue dress with white piping around the collar and sleeves, drove me in the Chevrolet the one-hundred-fifty miles to Durham, where I would begin college at North Carolina Central University.

We had purchased one black trunk to go with the three red suitcases that Mama had given me for my graduation present. Everything of meaning and usefulness to my life went into those four pieces of luggage–four dresses, two pairs of pants, the winter coat that I had worn for two years already, a sweater, new underwear, two sets of pajamas, two pairs of shoes, a pillow, sheets, towels, a new blue cotton bedspread, school supplies, and an old iron that Mama did not need anymore. In the red overnight case I put my hair rollers, a can of Aquanet hair spray, a full array of drug store makeup, and a small bonnet hair dryer. I was set. I knew that I would not be returning home to live again. This was expected of me at seventeen and I expected it of myself.

And there we were on that Sunday in September taking me off to start college. I would be the first person in either of my parents' entire families to ever go to a four-year university.

I was thrilled to be going to a place where I would be with other black people. N.C.C.U. is one of North Carolina's traditionally black universities. I believed that any and all race issues (a naïve belief I would later learn) would be resolved by my submerging myself in an absolutely all-black world. What of the larger South's interracial conflicts could intrude upon me there? I also believed that I might find my Mr. Right in that place and could begin to have those dozen kids that I dreamed of having. I was looking forward to my life ahead with great enthusiasm.

Mama delivered me to my room in Eagleson dormitory and after a quick meeting of my roommate, Vernolda Mack, she was gone.

I was on my own. I was finally the "grown-up" I had longed to be since early childhood. In those moments after Mama left, I felt both lonelier and freer than I had ever felt in my life before.

39

John and I arrive at my mother's Troy, North Carolina, home and park in the grass and gravel driveway. I stand in the yard of the house that Mama lived in for thirty years after I left for college. *So many years have passed since I left home carrying the trunk and the three red suitcases,* I think.

Memories of plastic Easter eggs hanging on the small bushes in Mama's yard come to mind. Over the previous thirty years, I had often visited in the spring, when the dogwoods were in bloom and when tree bark was fragrant from rain. The lily patch where Dale found my mother two days earlier seems too small for such a profound event as dying.

Mama moved herself and my younger brothers into this little house with her new husband after I left for college. I had never lived with her there.

John and I climb the two steps onto the squeaky grayed-wood porch, open the screen door, unlock the front door with the key Margo has given us and go inside. Entering Mama's house feels like entering a museum. The residual of burned tobacco is the backdrop for a laundry-pad perfumed smell.

Two sofas face one another. They have held all the people

that dropped by to see Mama without calling first. Shelves on the walls hold large framed pictures of all Mama's children in some phase of growing up. There is a collection of ceramic Avon pieces. A coffee table holds *Reader's Digests*, a *Woman's Day* magazine and the previous week's *Montgomery Herald*. A mantle over a closed-in fireplace holds candles and two small plastic rose arrangements.

Every object seems sacred. Every object holds information about the person that has collected and displayed it. How could there be so much value in the tulip lampshade that I had thought cheap in visits past? I am astounded by the respect I feel for the detritus of my mother's life. The need for more time with Mama's things than I know I have on my short visit to Troy fills me yet again.

On one wall of Mama's living room are pictures of both her husbands–my father Rob Gaddy and my half-brother Lewis' father. I study both pictures. My father stands beside the peach trees of Candor on sandy soil in a white shirt, tie, dress pants and dress shoes wearing a Stetson hat. He looks mellowed and confident. This was when my parents were courting, before marriage.

I look at her second husband's picture and wonder how much happier she may have been with him than with my father. The two men filled two thirds of my mother's adult life. The final third she was on her own, an independence that seemed, from my limited view, to suit her.

Thirty years in one place, in one home, in one town. I could not imagine it. During those thirty years, I traveled about the continent exploring and living in various parts of the United States and for one year, in Canada.

From her base in Troy, Mama gave birth to her last son, received one son back from the army, sent two children off to college, and said goodbye to me as I traveled three thousand miles across the country to live in Los Angeles. From that house, she launched Frankie out to live with me in the City of the Angels when he was sixteen and in trouble with the law. From there, she lived while four of her children married, me twice. After my half brother was off at college, she went back and forth daily to her job as manager at Troy's Maxway Department Store.

Knowing that she was there in that one place may have been what allowed me to experiment in relationship-having with her. Knowing where home was and would be, had given me a sense of security in life. Even if Mama did not respond to my letters or initiate calls to me, I always knew that she was where I now stood. I had been confident that she would never be going anywhere.

Along the way of my life away from my mother, away from Montgomery County, I learned that relationships could, even should be, reciprocal. Give and take. I give something into the relationship and the other person gives something. We grow it together. Two people intentionally and actively build a connection to one another.

Along the way, I tried to shift my tenth-grade-educated mother along with my awakenings. By giving gifts of stationary, rolls of postage stamps, telephone calling cards, I attempted to cajole Mama into reciprocal activity. She had none of this. After all, her mother, my grandmother Lena did not write to her. Grandma Lena was illiterate, so a mom-daughter letter exchange had not been one of my mother's experiences.

As we did not have a telephone while I was growing up, nor did Grandma Lena, my mother and her mother did not engage in chats via that avenue. As I recall, my mother saw her mother three or four times over the eighteen years of my childhood and they lived only sixty miles apart. This was my mother's norm. How could I have expected her to change, to become reciprocal even with literacy, telephones and air travel?

I shared a self help book once with Mama–*My Mother/My Self*. What did she have to say? "You live your life out of a book." The comment hurt. Reading self help books and going to therapists for advice was not something that interested my mother. I never broke through to her. I knew that she loved me, and I was certain that she knew I loved her. But there was so much judgment between us. Her old-timey ways and my educated, new-fangled ways.

As well as I could figure, she believed that the children in the family, once grown, should come back and see the mother. They should initiate the contacts, they should honor the matriarch of the family by giving without expecting reciprocity. *Honor thy father and thy mother: so that thy days may be long upon the land which the Lord Thy God giveth thee.* As an adult, I was not around to participate in the honoring of the matriarch.

Thanksgiving, eighteen months earlier, was our last visit.

Much like a wild rabbit flees at the sight of the hunter, I ran after seeing Mama. On my last day in her home, the smell of cigarette smoke overpowered me. Her teeth, browned from nicotine, shocked me. The shape of her face seemed changed from oval to square. I feared that the physical changes foretold death. I was certain that the poison that she had absorbed into her body for over fifty years from continuous smoking had caught up with her.

The worst was the cough. If my eyes had been closed, I would have thought I was in the presence of a shaken bucket of gravel, but the sounds of rattling and popping came from inside her lungs. I was terrified by what I saw in my mother's face, in her smoky home and by the noise that I heard coming from her body. As clear a thought as any I had ever had was the awareness that my mother was dying before my eyes. That she was killing herself. I was an emotional coward. I could not bear the loneliness of it. On that visit, I began to ride the wave that kept me at a distance from those feelings and from Mama.

I retreated. I did not see her again. I did not call her, or she me. She did not write to me in those eighteen months. Most recently, just four or five weeks earlier, I had sent Mama both a 70th birthday card and a Mother's Day card—both with money tucked inside.

It was unusual for me to send two cards, two gifts, as I had usually combined the two occasions and sent one communication. This year I, for some reason, saw the two occasions distinctly. I was struck by the importance of one's own birth into the world versus giving birth to another.

Standing there in Mama's living room, I looked about for signs of the cards that I had sent. *Maybe they are still here,* I thought. Maybe, although I had not heard one word from her, she may have valued them enough to display one for a while. *Not reciprocity per se, but valuing her daughter's thoughts and gestures enough to display a card.*

But there were no cards. None on the mantle or the coffee table or the shelves. In the kitchen, there were none stuck with a magnet onto the refrigerator door or propped atop it. In her bedroom, there were none sitting on a dresser or dressing table. I looked inside drawers and there was not a bundle of letters in any of them. *How odd* I thought to myself. I did not find my card, but I also did not find my brothers' cards that I was certain had been given. Had she discarded the greetings? This woman, who hoarded unused-shoe and empty-costume jewelry boxes, did not save her childrens' greeting cards?

I struggled. Was it she or I who let the other go first? Was it she or I who attempted to control the relationship by withholding? I wished for reciprocity, give and take. I have no idea what she required or even whether it–our distant relationship—was an issue for her. Was she simply repeating the mother-daughter pattern that she had had with her mother? Was she just too busy with her own life? Could it be that she too believed we had endless time for our relationship to evolve? Or was our relationship a thing of the past for her?

When I had been in my mother's presence in my adult life, I knew that she loved me. As a child, I often felt her love rain down upon me—when she rose with me at night when I was sick, when she walked with me and my siblings in the woods when I was a little child, when we visited on the long laundry days of my youth. But when I was away from my mother physically for any length of time, she let me go too totally.

The truth is also that I always had to go from my mother's world, because it ungrounded me. The violence and alcohol in the early days, then later on, divergences in thoughts, values, experiences and beliefs. I had taken such a different path than she.

My first big leave was when I was eleven years old, when I went to live with and work for Mrs. Richardson. I stayed away for months at a stretch, and my mother did not need, or at least did not follow through on any need she may have had to connect with me. It had felt then as though I no longer existed to her. How could she have let me, a little girl, go so completely?

Still as I walked through my dead mother's house, I asked myself *why did Mama not write, send a card, or call me the last eighteen months of her life?* My loneliness for her was not new. I had cultivated it over a lifetime. I felt powerless to get her to hold on to me through time, space, distance. But it never felt right to be without her. It was like watching horror movies over and over and trying to master them by extinguishing before it was even felt, the fear that might arise within me. I tried for a lifetime to master the loneliness that arose from the disconnect with my mother by extinguishing it also. That extinguishing of emotion and all my

295

leaving had a price. The price was missing whatever of my mother's attention and affection there may have been available for me had I lived nearer or had I reached out to her more, regardless as to what she did.

Now there will be no more physical togetherness. For that I am heartbroken. But there will neither be any more pining for or manipulating to get my mother to reach out and touch me from a distance. From all that useless dancing I am free. In the end, we loved one another as best we could. And I will always remember that there was the gift of the three red suitcases.

ACKNOWLEDGEMENTS

I wish to thank everyone who has had a hand in the creation of this book, however big or small. I know that I will not remember everyone but I will give it my best try. If I have neglected to name someone, please forgive me. It has only to do with my mind's inability to hold every one of your names for the purpose of writing acknowledgements and is not a reflection of my value of your contribution.

Over the years, there have been many readers of pieces of this book or the entire manuscript. Joe Nunn, Kyle Fordyce-Lytle, Larry Wallace, Kenya Johnson, Victor Wolfenstein, Anna Batoosingh, Rosey Scurini, Virginia Hughes, Peggy Yeargain-Williams, Bernice Roberts, Susan Teed, Helen Neville, Carol Hughes. Thank you all for your loving support, feedback, reviews and encouragement. Thank you to other pre-publication reviewers: Loretta Ishida, Peter Likins, and Reggie Daniels. Gratitude to you, Nancy Brown, for your friendship over the past three-and-a-half decades and for writing the foreword to this book. Nancy Linnon and former members of our Tucson writer's group, thank you for being with me early on in the process of turning my childhood memories into art. June Davidson, thank you for remaining a close friend throughout the years since our writers' group and encouraging my every subsequent artistic endeavor with great enthusiasm and interest.

During this most recent phase of preparation for publishing, I wish to thank all those who have helped make this book, and me, ready for the public. Cynthia Couture, thank you for editing when I could not face the overwhelming task of doing so due to the big emotions I still felt about my childhood. Because of you, publishing began to feel manageable and I moved forward with gusto. Thank you Alice Sarog of Summer & Company Photography in Qualicum Beach, British Columbia, Canada, for the most beautiful photo session and pictures.

When I decided to narrate the audio book version of *Three Red Suitcases*, I did not know what I would be in for. Cory Woodward, Producer and Owner of Little Bear Music Co. in Nanaimo, British Columbia, and member of the most wonderful band *Lion Bear Fox*, I thank you. Your kindness, generosity, engagement and holding space for me as I spoke aloud my words was truly a profound experience.

To my brother, Lee Gaddy, your support of me speaking my truths is invaluable. For this and you, I feel deep gratitude.

Finally, to my husband of nearly thirty years—John Huntley, you are the glue that holds my crazy world together. Thank you for sharing my life, for your commitment to our journey together and your support of my dreams, no matter how inconvenient or disruptive at times. You are the "good husband" that I promised Mrs. Richardson that I was going to marry one day.

READING GROUP GUIDE

Three Red Suitcases Book Club meets on Facebook. Go to https://www.facebook.com/Levonnegaddysbook/ and press "Visit Group" button or you can also go to www.LevonneGaddy.com/ to connect.

If your book club wishes to read and discuss *Three Red Suitcases*, listed are some questions to help guide your group talk. A suggestion is that you choose five to ten questions around which to focus your discussion. Thank you.

1. How did you experience the book? Were you engaged immediately? How did you feel reading it?
2. What are the themes of the book?
3. What do you know about the history of interracial marriage in America? When were the first laws instituted? What were the reasons for interracial marriage being illegal? When did interracial marriage laws change in America? Under what laws were Levonne's grandparents married?
4. What are your thoughts and feelings about the circumstances under which Ovella was conceived?
5. Do you know about the one-drop rule related to

racial identity? How did this play out in Levonne's family?

6. What are your thoughts about fostering biracial or multiracial identity in children?

7. What attributes, qualities do you attach to a person's skin color? What attributes were attached to Levonne and her family member's skin color by themselves? By those outside their family?

8. Were you surprised by the events of Levonne's childhood as they unfolded? What was most surprising?

9. Does Levonne's family remind you of any families you know?

10. How would you describe Ovella and Rob's use of alcohol? How much do you think it contributed to the physical violence between Ovella and Rob?

11. How did the domestic partner abuse make you feel about Ovella and Rob?

12. What may have been the impact of domestic violence on Levonne and her siblings? Should the children have been removed from their parents, as Child Protective Services might remove children today for their own safety?

13. Do you know about FAS (Fetal Alcohol Syndrome)? What were your thoughts and feelings about Frankie being labeled as premature? His behavior of not learning from consequences? What did you think about how Frankie's behavior was handled by the family?

14. What were the skills and strategies Levonne used for coping with painful and stressful situations in her family? Can you think of better ways, given her circumstances, for her to have coped?

15. What role did nature play in Levonne's life?

16. What was your understanding of Levonne's relationship with her mother? Did the relationship seem common or abnormal to you?

17. How would you describe Levonne's feelings toward her father? What impact did his behaviors have on her and her relationships with others?

18. How would today's culture judge Levonne's parents for allowing her to leave home at age eleven to work? What do you think and how do you feel about it?

19. Is it possible for a child to "go to work" too early in life? What might be residual fallout from a child's non-age-appropriate entry into the work world? What circumstances might make going to work at an early age okay or not okay?

20. What factors contributed to Levonne's resiliency?

21. What are your thoughts about racial segregation and integration of schools? Did school integration work for Levonne? Why or why not?

22. What did you think about the contrast between the way Mrs. McAlister taught Levonne and the way Mr. Keith taught her?

23. How important are friendships in a child's life?

Was Levonne scarred emotionally by loosing friends in the 7th grade?

24. What did you think and feel about Levonne and Mrs. Richardson's relationship?

25. Was Mrs. Richardson racist? How so, or not? What was your emotional response to her?

26. What do you think about the shifting dynamic in the family when Lee began standing up to his father and asserting himself?

27. When Levonne was sexually assaulted, how did you react? What did you want her to do in response to the act? Do you know someone that was raped as a child? How does a child recover from sexual assault if they keep it a secret?

28. What was your response to how Levonne handled her father's death?

29. Do you think it was the best decision for Levonne to return home to her mother and brothers after her father's death?

30. How did adult Levonne resolve her feelings about the distance between her and her mother in the final chapter of the book? Did she resolve her feelings?

31. If you could ask the author, adult Levonne, one question now, what would it be?

32. Do you think the name of the book fit? Why or why not?

33. Has this childhood memoir changed you or taught you anything?

ABOUT THE AUTHOR

LEVONNE GADDY, writer, artist, "world citizen", is a native North Carolinian and graduated North Carolina Central University and University of California Los Angeles. She authored four books, numerous newspaper articles, and blogs.

Today, Levonne divides her time between Vancouver Island, British Columbia, Canada and San Carlos, Sonora, Mexico. She resides with her partner of three decades and their two spaniels. Her major joys in life are creating art, writing, exploring the science of consciousness, communing with good friends and preparing plant-based meals.

You can contact Levonne and discover resources for writing a memoir and for recovery from childhood trauma at her website, www.LevonneGaddy.com

To see other books written by Levonne, go to her Amazon Author page, https://www.amazon.com/-/e/B00BQ6778U